Nick Vandome

Smart
Homes

in easy steps

In easy steps is an imprint of In Easy Steps Limited
16 Hamilton Terrace · Holly Walk · Leamington Spa
Warwickshire · United Kingdom · CV32 4LY
www.ineasysteps.com

Notice of Liability

Every effort has been made to ensure that this book contains accurate
and current information. However, In Easy Steps Limited and the
author shall not be liable for any loss or damage suffered by readers
as a result of any information contained herein.

Trademarks

All trademarks are acknowledged as belonging to their respective
companies.

In Easy Steps Limited supports The Forest Stewardship Council (FSC),
the leading international forest certification organization. All our titles
that are printed on Greenpeace approved FSC certified paper carry the
FSC logo.

MIX
Paper from
responsible sources
FSC® C020837

Printed and bound in the United Kingdom

ISBN 978-1-84078-825-9

Contents

1 About Smart Homes

This chapter introduces the concept of the smart home and shows some of the uses for smart home devices.

Introducing the Smart Home

The concept of the smart home, i.e. one in which most of the electronic devices are controlled via voice controls, apps, or accessed remotely, is not a science fiction vision of the future; it is very much part of the here and now, and a realistic and affordable option for most households. For a smart home to work to its full potential there are a number of elements that can be in place:

- Smart home devices.

- Digital voice assistants, or hubs.

- Apps on smartphones and tablets, and online access.

Smart homes can operate without all three of these elements; e.g. smart home devices can be operated without digital voice assistants or apps, but to get the complete smart home experience, it is worth having all three in place.

Range of devices

Also known as the Internet of Things (IoT), smart home technology now spans a wide range of devices (and this is increasing regularly) as manufacturers realize the commercial importance of smart homes. Some of the current devices are:

Don't forget

Some people consider smart home devices to be an irrelevance that automates tasks that are already easily done manually. However, similar things were said when the television remote control was first introduced. The range of functionality for smart home devices ensures that it is likely that they will become as common in the home as the ubiquitous TV remote.

Don't forget

Smart home devices use a range of methods of wireless communication to link to their related apps or remote controls. The most common is Wi-Fi, but various devices also use Bluetooth, Zigbee and Z-Wave. These are looked at on page 13.

- **Smart lighting systems**, including smart light bulbs and a bridge that connects to your Wi-Fi router. Individual lights can be controlled around the home with an app, a digital voice assistant, or a remote control. Groups of lights can also be used to create artistic effects. Smart lighting apps contain a range of settings that can be used to give you maximum control and flexibility over your lighting system.

PHILIPS
Hue white and color

- **Smart thermostats**.
  Heating systems can be
  controlled to turn them
  on and off and set the
  temperature. They can
  also be used to determine
  whether there are people
  at home, and regulate the
  temperature accordingly.
  In this way, they can be
  used to save money on
  your heating bills.

Smart home devices
can also operate in the
traditional manual way,
in case their wireless
communication is not
working. For instance,
smart light bulbs can be
operated using the usual
wall switch, and a smart
heating system can still
be controlled using the
manual control panel.

- **Smart security systems**. Extensive security systems, using
  external cameras, can be installed, and controlled and viewed
  via an app.

- **Smart locks**. In addition to security cameras, smart locks can
  be used to add additional security to your home. They can be
  activated by key cards, key fobs, apps, digital voice assistants,
  time-limited PIN codes, and even remotely.

- **Smart cameras**.
  Individual cameras
  can be used within
  the home, such as
  for monitoring a
  baby's bedroom,
  or the outside of a
  property.

There are also an
increasing number of
miscellaneous smart
home devices, such as
smart kettles, smart
blinds, smart humidifiers
and smart portable air
conditioners. The list of
smart home devices will
undoubtedly expand as
the technology becomes
more widely available.

- **Smart plugs and sockets**. Individual smart plugs can be used
  throughout the home, so that devices can be turned on and
  off without having to physically press a switch.

- **Robotic lawnmowers and cleaners**. Tasks within or outside
  the home can be automated through the use of robot lawn
  mowers, vacuum cleaners and mops. These do not all have
  their own compatible apps, but can work independently.

...cont'd

Digital voice assistants

Digital voice assistants are fast becoming the must-have accessory in the digital world. They consist of a stand-alone speaker, with the functionality provided by the digital voice assistant, which provides information from the cloud via your home Wi-Fi.

Digital voice assistants can perform a range of tasks such as providing news updates, telling a joke, playing music, and controlling smart home devices.

Different manufacturers have their own digital voice assistants, and the main ones are (the speaker is first, with the digital voice assistant second):

- The Amazon Echo and Alexa.

- The Google Home and Google Assistant.

- The Apple HomePod and Siri.

For each device the functionality is similar: the speaker connects to your home Wi-Fi and any requests for information are then sent to the cloud service for the relevant device. For instance, if you ask the Google Assistant to tell you the weather for the following day, the details will come from Google, in the same way as for searching with Google on the web. For smart home devices, instructions can be given to the digital voice assistant, and these will be actioned via your home Wi-Fi and the Wi-Fi functionality of the smart home device.

Hot tip

It is possible to combine separate digital voice assistants with your smart devices. For instance, you can control them from the Amazon Echo and Alexa, and also with Siri on your iPhone or iPad, using the Home apps on these devices.

10

Digital voice assistants also have associated apps, where settings can be applied for the device; e.g. the Alexa app for the Echo and Alexa, the Google Home app for Google Home and the Google Assistant, and the Home app for the Apple HomePod and Siri. Depending on the device, there is a considerable range of settings that can be applied with the associated app.

☰	Settings	
Music & Media		>
Flash Briefing		>
Traffic		>
Sports Update		>
Calendar		>
Lists		>

Smart home apps

Although it is not essential to use apps with smart home devices, it rather defeats the purpose of them if this valuable option is ignored. Most smart home devices have a companion app that can be used to control the device, either in the home, or remotely. Remote access can require registering with the device's related website; e.g. if you are using the Philips Hue smart lighting system, you can register at the Philips website and then control your lighting system when you are away from home.

Smart home apps offer significant functionality, depending on the type of smart home device, and some of the options include:

- Turning devices on and off.

- Using preset scenes (for devices such as smart lighting) to create a variety of color combinations.

- Setting timers so that devices turn on and off at specific times; e.g. set smart heating to come on in the morning and turn off in the evening, and also a variety of times in between.

- Creating customized routines to give ultimate control over your smart home devices.

Hot tip

Digital voice assistants have to be linked to a compatible service in order for them to communicate with a smart device. This is similar to adding an app on a smartphone or tablet.

11

Controlling Smart Devices

Most smart home devices perform tasks that we have traditionally done by physically interacting with the devices. However, smart home functionality now means that there are several ways that we can interact with devices around the home and control them.

Manual control

For anyone nervous about the prospect of smart home devices becoming inactive due to a technological breakdown (or worse, being hacked and controlled by a malicious agent), it is important to note that most smart home devices can be controlled manually, without any need for wireless connectivity. For instance, smart lights can be turned on and off by hand, without any concern about the wireless technology that they contain. This means that if, for instance, your Wi-Fi is not available, you can still control the majority of the smart devices in your home. Similarly, if you have security concerns about unwanted access to your devices, you could turn off your Wi-Fi and still be able to use your smart home devices, but without much of their smart functionality.

App control

Smart home devices have their own companion apps that can be used on smartphones and tablets to control the devices. This is usually done via a reasonably straightforward interface where devices can be turned on or off, or have timing schedules applied for them, and a variety of general settings.

Digital voice assistants

Digital voice assistants, such as Amazon's Alexa, Google's Google Assistant and Apple's Siri, can be used for a variety of tasks, including controlling smart home devices. This is done by enabling the digital voice assistant with the equivalent of an app on a smartphone or tablet, and then using this to control smart home devices with voice commands. Not all smart home devices are compatible with digital voice assistants, but it is something that is being included with an increasing range of devices.

Smart home hubs

Digital voice assistants act as hubs to control smart home devices. Similarly, there are hubs that are designed specifically for this task, without the additional functionality of a digital voice assistant. These hubs can be used to connect and control a wide range of smart home devices, using the hub's companion app.

Like all computing devices, security for smart home devices is an important issue. For more details about this, see pages 16-20.

Connectivity for Devices

Smart home devices communicate wirelessly with the app, hub or digital voice assistant that is instructing them with commands. However, different devices use various methods of wireless communication to achieve this. These include:

- **Wi-Fi**. This is a well-known method of wireless communication, due mainly to its role in connecting computing devices wirelessly to the internet. However, it is increasingly being used to connect smart home devices. This is usually done with a bridge that connects to your home Wi-Fi router. The smart home device's app, hub or digital voice assistant can then communicate with the device, via the bridge that is connected to the Wi-Fi router.

- **Z-Wave**. This is a method of wireless communication that was developed in 2001, specifically for use with smart home devices. It enables Z-Wave devices to communicate directly with an app, hub or digital voice assistant, without the need for a bridge connected to a Wi-Fi router.

- **Zigbee**. This is another method of wireless communication designed to operate over relatively short distances, and is therefore well suited to smart home devices. It is similar to Bluetooth communication in its operation but intended to have simpler technological requirements. It operates by allowing apps, hubs and digital voice assistants to connect wirelessly to Zigbee-enabled devices, creating a personal area network between the smart home device and the method of connecting to it (app, hub or digital voice assistant).

- **Bluetooth**. A well-established method of wireless communication over short distances, Bluetooth can be used to connect a range of peripherals to computing devices. It can also be used to connect smart home devices, although many manufacturers of these devices lean towards Wi-Fi or one of the wireless communication methods that are designed specifically for smart home devices.

Don't forget

If devices connect directly to an app on a smartphone or a tablet, without the need for a Wi-Fi bridge, you may not be aware of the type of connectivity used by the device. However, this should be listed in any documentation that comes with the device.

Day in the Life of a Smart Home

Everyone will use smart home devices in different ways, and this will probably evolve over time as more devices are added. Here are some examples of what you could do in your smart home:

Morning

- Wake up to the smart lighting coming on automatically.

- Ask for a news and weather update from your digital voice assistant.

- Turn on the heating from your smartphone or tablet, using the smart heating app.

- Open the curtains/drapes with an app on your smartphone or tablet.

- Ask your digital voice assistant to boil your smart kettle for a breakfast cup of coffee.

Afternoon

- Use the smart vacuum cleaner to clean your home.

- Answer the front door to someone, using a smart video doorbell, so that you can see the caller at the door.

- Turn on a smart plug that is connected to a robotic lawnmower to cut the grass automatically.

- Get a traffic update from your digital voice assistant before you go out.

- Set the smart heating system to Eco setting when you go out.

Beware

Before buying any smart home device, ask yourself if it will really make a difference to your home, and the way that you interact with it, rather than just being a gimmick that is rarely used after the initial novelty of it.

14

Hot tip

Smart heating systems can be set up so that they can recognize when there is no one at home and apply the Eco setting accordingly.

Evening

- Turn on all the lights in your home with a single tap on an app or a voice command for your digital voice assistant.

- Set a lighting scene for a room that has colored smart light bulbs, to create colored combinations.

Hot tip

Smart home devices such as smart heating and smart lighting can have schedules applied to them so that they are turned on and off at specific times.

- Check that all smart locks are shut, using the smart lock app, or digital voice assistant.

- Check that all electrical devices are off, using the smart plug app, or digital voice assistant.

- Turn off the heating with the smart heating app, or digital voice assistant.

- Check the smart security camera system before you go to bed.

- Turn off all the lights with the smart lighting app, or digital voice assistant.

Security Issues

How secure is the smart home?

Computing devices are inherently insecure to a certain extent and prone to malicious attacks, if the perpetrator is persistent enough. This is an ongoing problem with personal computers and larger commercial computing systems. But what does it mean in terms of security for the smart home? As with any system that relies on computing devices, there is the potential for hackers to gain access to smart home devices and apps that control them. However, smart home technology is still at a relatively early stage of development and security will undoubtedly become more of an imperative as smart homes gain a greater foothold within the mainstream consumer market. Some general areas of smart home security are:

- **App security**. Smart home devices are usually linked to companion apps that can be used to control the devices. However, to do this they are granted a range of permissions that influence the functionality of the device, such as being able to open and close a smart lock that is securing your home. If hackers gain access to these apps then it could have considerable security implications, as they will be able to control access to your home. The best way to mitigate against this is to ensure your smart home apps are as up-to-date as possible and that you install any software and security updates that become available for the apps.

- **Wireless security**. Almost all smart devices derive their functionality from some form of wireless communication; e.g. Wi-Fi or Bluetooth. There are also some newer wireless protocols that are designed specifically for use with smart home devices. As with all digital communications, there is potential for hackers to intercept wireless communications (through any security flaws) and use this to gain access to your smart home devices. Wi-Fi is one of the most common ways to connect to smart home devices, so it is important that you protect your home Wi-Fi router as well as you can.

- **Integrated systems**. Some manufacturers offer integrated smart home systems, where one system is used to control all of the smart home devices. The obvious risk here is if hackers gain access to the system then they can control everything in your smart home.

Don't forget

Attacks on smart home devices are not unheard of, but they are relatively rare. It is a personal decision to weigh up the security risks against the range of benefits that smart home devices offer.

Secure your Wi-Fi

For the majority of homes with smart devices the main method of communicating with these devices will be through your home Wi-Fi network; i.e. the one that you use to connect to the internet. Therefore it is important that your Wi-Fi network is as secure as possible. This starts with the Wi-Fi router, and there are some areas that should be considered when using a router.

- **Firewall**. A Wi-Fi router that uses a recognized firewall should be used as this will help to prevent malicious software and programs infecting your system.

- **Encryption**. This should be used by your router, to ensure that all communication is encrypted to make it much harder to be hacked or intercepted.

- **Auto-updating**. Routers sometimes have software updates that are designed to improve security or patch any flaws that have been identified. Look for a router that does this automatically whenever an update is available.

One area of security weakness for Wi-Fi routers can be their admin password. This is set when the router is manufactured and is generally very basic, along the lines of "admin" or "password". It is therefore important to change this password as soon as possible, to make it more secure. To do this:

1 Open a web browser and type the router's address in the address bar. (This is usually in a form similar to 192.168.1.1 or similar. Check with the documentation that came with the router, or search on the web using your router's model name)

2 Enter the **Username** and **Password**. If these have never been changed they should be along the lines of Admin and Password

Login

Enter your username and password to access your Technicolor Gateway.

Username: admin

Password: ●●●●●●●●●●●

OK   Cancel

Check the specifications of a router to see what it offers in terms of a firewall, encryption and auto-updating.

17

Keep a look out for any strange behavior from your smart home devices, such as smart lights turning on or off when they are not instructed to, or flashing unexpectedly, as this could be a sign that your devices have been hacked or are being controlled remotely by someone else.

...cont'd

3 The Admin options are displayed. These should include items relating to your internet connection and a toolbox for changing admin settings

18

4 Within the Toolbox, locate the option for changing the password

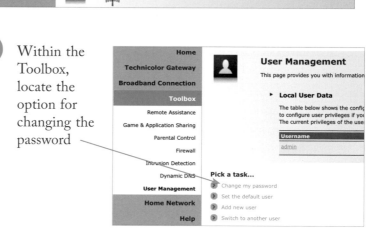

5 Enter the current password (old password), enter the new password, confirm it and tap on the **Change Password** button

Always listening

Smart speakers and digital voice assistants such as Amazon Echo and Alexa, Google Home and Assistant, and Apple HomePod and Siri are increasingly becoming integral elements in our homes, and they contribute to a range of functionality in the smart home.

Digital voice assistants work by listening to your conversations and then acting on specific commands that are preceded by the device's "wake word". The digital voice assistant will also record commands that are preceded by the wake word and store the information on the device's server; i.e. the device manufacturer's computer that is linked to the device. For instance, if you use the Amazon Echo, recorded commands are stored on an Amazon computer. Since the digital voice assistant is always ready to respond to commands, it means that it is always listening, and just waiting until it hears the wake word.

Since digital voice assistants are always listening, it can cause some issues if it thinks it has heard a wake word, when that has not been the case. There have been some instances where a digital voice assistant has misinterpreted a conversation, thinking that it contains the wake word. The device then listened to the conversation and mistakenly sent a recorded message to a contact in its address book, without the person who was engaged in the original conversation being aware of its action. Although this is a rare occurrence, it is important to remember that your digital voice assistant is always listening and to bear this in mind if you are discussing sensitive information such as personal financial details. Some areas of conversation to consider if you are concerned about your digital voice assistant overhearing it are:

- Personal information and details relating to your family members and friends.

- Financial information, such as bank account details.

- Passwords and PIN codes for online websites, and also physical items such as bank credit and debit cards.

- Anything you would not feel comfortable with if it were distributed to a wider audience.

If in doubt, turn off your digital voice assistant before you have a conversation about a particular subject.

Beware

Digital voice assistants can also be inadvertently activated if they hear their wake word on the TV or radio.

...cont'd

It is possible to view details of everything that a digital voice assistant has recorded, usually within the device's companion app's settings. To do this (this example is for the Amazon Alexa):

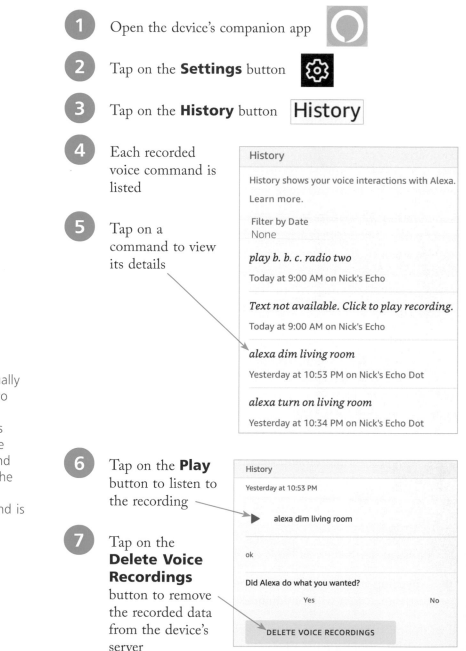

1 Open the device's companion app

2 Tap on the **Settings** button

3 Tap on the **History** button History

4 Each recorded voice command is listed

5 Tap on a command to view its details

History

History shows your voice interactions with Alexa. Learn more.

Filter by Date
None

play b. b. c. radio two
Today at 9:00 AM on Nick's Echo

Text not available. Click to play recording.
Today at 9:00 AM on Nick's Echo

alexa dim living room
Yesterday at 10:53 PM on Nick's Echo Dot

alexa turn on living room
Yesterday at 10:34 PM on Nick's Echo Dot

6 Tap on the **Play** button to listen to the recording

7 Tap on the **Delete Voice Recordings** button to remove the recorded data from the device's server

History

Yesterday at 10:53 PM

▶ alexa dim living room

ok

Did Alexa do what you wanted?

Yes   No

DELETE VOICE RECORDINGS

Don't forget

Voice recordings usually start a second or two before the actual voice command. This is because the device is always listening and records just before the command to ensure that the full command is captured.

2 About Digital Voice Assistants

Digital voice assistants can be used to control a range of smart home devices, and this chapter gives an overview of getting started with them.

Digital Voice Assistants

Digital voice assistants initially became popular in mainstream computing when they were introduced on smartphones, and then tablets. This enabled users to ask a range of questions using the mobile devices, without having to physically type in the request. This is achieved by using data stored in the digital voice assistant's connected cloud service; e.g. information stored on a computer server that can be accessed by the digital voice assistant. So, when a voice request such as "What is the weather like in Kathmandu today?" is made, the reply is generated from information held on the web, in the same way as typing a request into a search engine on a PC, laptop, smartphone or tablet.

Digital voice assistants in the home

Recognizing the value of digital voice assistants, the major technology companies were quick to recognize the benefit of developing these types of devices for widespread use in the home. This has resulted in the rapid rise of smart speakers for the home: speakers that connect to your Wi-Fi network and then harness the connected digital voice assistant. This can then be used for an increasing range of tasks: from playing music to controlling your smart home devices. The speakers and the digital voice assistants should be considered as separate entities, and they both have their own names. The three main smart speakers are produced by three of the technology giants:

22

Don't forget

For more information about setting up and using Amazon's Alexa, see Chapter 3; for the Google Assistant, see Chapter 4; and for Apple's Siri, see Chapter 5.

- **Amazon,** with the Echo speaker that uses Alexa as its digital voice assistant. There is a range of Echo speakers that come in various sizes and can perform different tasks. For instance, the Echo Spot has a screen that can be used to make video calls and also view movies and TV shows from a streaming service such as Amazon Video or Netflix.

● **Google**, with the Google Home speaker that uses the Google Assistant as its digital voice assistant. In addition to the standard model, there is also a Google Mini version, so that the system can be used in different rooms around the home.

● **Apple**, with the HomePod speaker that uses Siri as its digital voice assistant. This is the most expensive of the three digital voice assistants but, like the other two, has excellent sound quality from the speaker.

Don't forget

The digital voice assistant that you use may depend on other digital devices that you own. For instance, if you have an iPhone and an iPad you may favor the HomePod. However, all of these devices have their own apps so that they can be operated from different digital devices, regardless of their operating system.

Using Digital Voice Assistants

Digital voice assistants can be used to control a range of smart home devices (through wireless communication). In addition, they can add their own smart home functionality by enabling you to perform a range of tasks using voice commands. These include:

- News and sports updates.

- Weather information.

- The latest traffic news for specific routes.

- Playing music that you have made available to your digital voice assistant.

- Listening to the radio.

- Recipes.

Adding skills/actions

These options are pre-installed to a digital voice assistant, so that they are available as soon as it has been set up. However, it is also possible to increase the functionality of a digital voice assistant by adding skills/actions. This is similar to adding an app to a smartphone or tablet so that more tasks can be performed.

Skills/actions are added through the digital voice assistant's companion app (see next page) and there is a section where all of the available skills/actions can be viewed.

Don't forget

There is no reason why you cannot use more than one digital voice assistant in your home. However, it makes more sense to select one system and use this throughout your home, as required.

Setting up

Setting up a digital voice assistant, and adding skills/actions to increase its functionality, has to be done by an app on a smartphone or a tablet. This will enable the digital voice assistant to be connected to your home Wi-Fi network, so that it can then access all of the required content from its linked cloud server. The Google and Apple digital voice assistants usually have the relevant apps (Google Home and Home) pre-installed on their respective smartphones and tablets. For Amazon's Alexa, the Alexa app has to be downloaded to a smartphone or tablet, from either the Apple App Store or the Google Play Store.

The general process for setting up a digital voice assistant is:

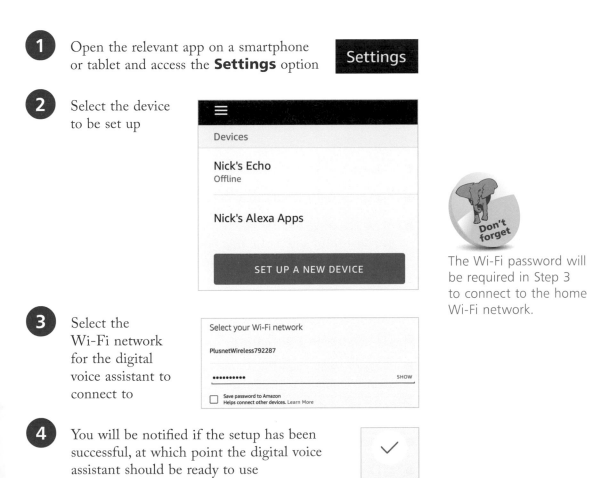

1 Open the relevant app on a smartphone or tablet and access the **Settings** option

2 Select the device to be set up

Devices

Nick's Echo
Offline

Nick's Alexa Apps

SET UP A NEW DEVICE

3 Select the Wi-Fi network for the digital voice assistant to connect to

Select your Wi-Fi network

PlusnetWireless792287

•••••••••• SHOW

☐ Save password to Amazon
Helps connect other devices. Learn More

4 You will be notified if the setup has been successful, at which point the digital voice assistant should be ready to use

All done!

The Wi-Fi password will be required in Step 3 to connect to the home Wi-Fi network.

Functionality

Digital voice assistants require a "wake word" to enable them to activate a request. This is to avoid them being activated accidentally simply by someone saying something like, "I wonder what the weather will be like tomorrow".

Wake words can be changed for some digital voice assistants, but the default ones are:

- "Alexa…", for Alexa on the Amazon Echo.

- "Okay Google…", or "Hey Google…", for Google Assistant on the Google Home.

- "Hey Siri…", for Siri on the Apple HomePod.

Whatever device and wake word that is used, the three main digital voice assistants can all perform a variety of tasks in response to voice commands. These include:

- "[Device wake word], what time is it?"

- "[Device wake word], what is the current weather?" (This is based on the location specified during the setup of the device.)

- "[Device wake word], will it rain tomorrow?"

- "[Device wake word], play radio station XXX."

- "[Device wake word], play [selected music or artist]." (This is taken from any music that is stored in the music library linked to the digital voice assistant, or a music streaming service, if one has been set up.)

- "[Device wake word], stop."

- "[Device wake word], pause."

- "[Device wake word], volume up/down" or "[Device wake word], volume [1-10]."

- "[Device wake word], tell me a joke."

- "[Device wake word], set a timer for XX minutes."

- "[Device wake word], what is the definition of [selected word]?"

Don't forget

If a digital voice assistant cannot understand a command it will tell you immediately.

- "[Device wake word], tell me the news." (This can be customized with different news providers, and there is also usually an option to receive a news briefing that contains news and sports updates from a range of different news content providers.)

- "[Device wake word], how do you say [selected word] in [selected language]?"

- "[Device wake word], what is the square root of 81?"

- "[Device wake word], what is that capital of [country]?"

- "[Device wake word], what movies are playing nearby?" (This is based on the location specified during the setup of the device.)

- "[Device wake word], list Chinese restaurants nearby." (This is based on location, as above.)

- "[Device wake word], help", to get details of the type of help questions that can be asked; e.g. "[Device wake word], how do I connect to Bluetooth?"

- "[Device wake word], how many kilometers in a mile?"

- "[Device wake word], how many grams in an ounce?"

- "[Device wake word], how many US dollars to the UK pound?"

- "[Device wake word], give me a recipe for [selected dish]."

- "[Device wake word], give me a tip."

- "[Device wake word], turn on the bedroom light."

- "[Device wake word], turn off the heating."

For some of the functionality for digital voice assistants the information can be taken directly from the cloud content that is linked to the device; for instance, for news and weather. For other items such as tips or random facts, or controlling smart home devices, skills/actions will have to be downloaded on the device's companion app to provide this specific functionality for the digital voice assistant.

Beware

The way in which a request is made can sometimes affect the response. For instance, if you say "[Device wake word], turn the bedroom light to on", this may not be recognized. Instead, the phrase, "[Device wake word], turn on the bedroom lights" may provide the desired response from the digital voice assistant.

Using IFTTT

IFTTT stands for If That Then This, which is a functionality whereby an action can be used to trigger one, or more, additional actions. This is done using the IFTTT app, or the IFTTT website, and it can be used to create hundreds of interactions between apps, social media sites and digital voice assistants such as Amazon Alexa, Google Assistant, and Apple Siri. IFTTT is a great way to perform a number of tasks with a single command. To use IFTTT:

Hot tip

In addition to being used with digital voice assistants, IFTTT functionality can also be used on smartphones and tablets. For instance, photos on an iPhone can be organized into folders using an IFTTT applet, and contacts can be backed up into a Google Docs document.

1 Download the IFTTT app from the Apple App Store or the Google Play Store

2 You can sign in to IFTTT with either a Google account or a Facebook account, or you can create an IFTTT account by tapping on the **sign up** button

Get started with **IFTTT**

G Continue with Google

f Continue with Facebook

Or use email to sign up or sign in

3 The functionality for IFTTT is provided by small programs called applets (small apps). There are hundreds of options that can be used with a wide range of devices and services. Tap on the **Discover** button on the bottom toolbar to view the featured options

Q Discover

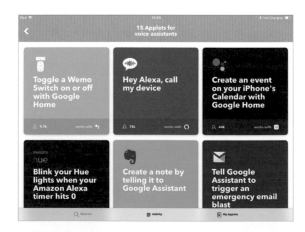

4 Tap on an applet to use its functionality with your digital voice assistant (there is no need to add anything through your digital voice assistant's own app)

5 Tap on the **Turn on** button to activate the applet

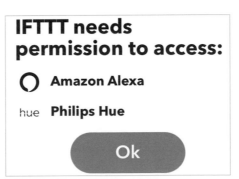

Hot tip

IFTTT applets are excellent for working with social media sites. For instance, you can use an applet to publish photos to all of your social media sites, just by publishing them to one site – the applet then automatically sends them to your other sites.

29

6 For each applet, you need to give permission for it to access the devices and/or services used in providing the functionality. Tap on the **Ok** button to do this

IFTTT needs permission to access:

○ **Amazon Alexa**

hue **Philips Hue**

Ok

...cont'd

7 Allow each item to have access to IFTTT in order for it to perform the applet's functionality

IFTTT would like access to:

ⓘ **IFTTT**

Name: Nick Vandome
Email address: nickvandome@mac.com
Access to your Alexa information (like To-do lists) to trigger recipes you create.
Permission to publish information to, and write and modify information on, Alexa in order to execute recipes you create.

Allow

PHILIPS

hue *personal wireless lighting*

English ∨   Sign out

Hue account

Grant permission to IFTTT

IFTTT is requesting access to control and monitor your Philips Hue system over the internet. This application will have access to your lights, switches and sensors.

Do you trust this application?

Yes   No

Beware

Each time you select a new device or service, you will need to give it permission to access and use the IFTTT app.

8 Preview the applet's functionality, and tap on the **Save** button to install it

Blink your Hue lights when your Amazon Alexa timer hits 0

Add some visual flair to your countdown. Tip: this is a great Applet if you or someone else in the home is hearing impaired.

Receive notifications when this Applet runs

hue

Philips Hue

Blink lights
This Action will briefly turn your hue lights off then back on.

Which lights?

All lights   ∨

Save

Searching for IFTTT applets

There are hundreds of applets within the IFTTT app, and they can be searched for using specific criteria; i.e. for a device, or a service offered by another app. To find IFTTT applets:

1 Tap on the **Discover** button on the bottom toolbar

2 Tap on the search icon on the top toolbar to search for specific applets

3 Enter the search criteria in the Search box

4 Applets that match the search criteria are shown under the **Applets** tab

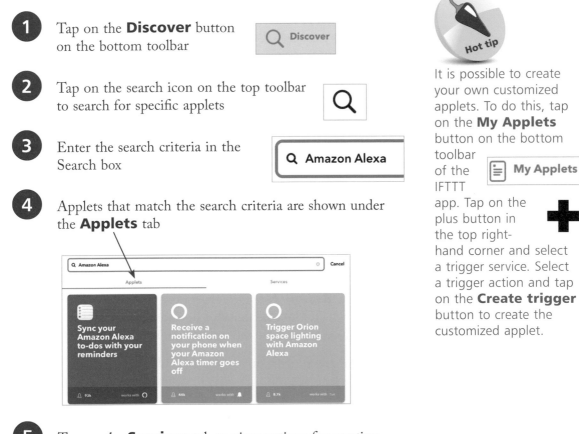

5 Tap on the **Services** tab to view options for creating IFTTT actions for linking to apps and online services

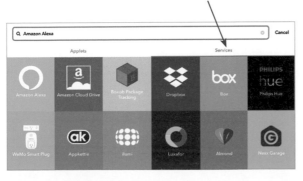

Hot tip

It is possible to create your own customized applets. To do this, tap on the **My Applets** button on the bottom toolbar of the IFTTT app. Tap on the plus button in the top right-hand corner and select a trigger service. Select a trigger action and tap on the **Create trigger** button to create the customized applet.

Digital Voice Assistant Apps

Digital voice assistants can be set up and controlled via their companion apps. The apps can be used on a range of devices to control digital voice assistants, even if they are not linked directly to the device. For instance, the Alexa app can be downloaded from the Apple App Store onto an iPhone and this can then be used to set up an Amazon Echo and activate Alexa. Similarly, the Google Home app can be used on Apple and Google mobile devices (using the iOS and Android operating systems respectively).

The apps for the different digital voice assistants are:

- **Alexa app for Alexa on the Amazon Echo**. This can be used on an iOS and an Android mobile device. The app can be used to set up and apply settings to Alexa. It can also be used to add skills for Alexa, to expand its functionality.

- **Google Home app for Google Assistant on the Google Home**. This can be used on an iOS and Android mobile device. It can be used to connect to a Google Home device and apply settings for it. There is a separate Google Assistant app that can be used to add Google Assistant to a mobile device such as a smartphone or a tablet.

- **Home app for Siri on the HomePod**. This is only available on iOS mobile devices; i.e. the iPhone, iPad and iPod Touch. Siri can also be set up on an iPhone, an iPad, or an iPod Touch within the Settings app.

All three apps for their respective digital voice assistants can be used to control a range of smart home devices. For instance, if you install a smart lighting system, the smart light bulbs can be set up in the digital voice assistant's app, and then controlled via the assistant itself. The functionality of smart home devices can also be controlled from within the digital voice assistant's app.

Beware

Each digital voice assistant and its companion app operate in slightly different ways. The Alexa app contains the greatest range of options in terms of applying settings and options for Alexa on the Echo. The Google Home app is used to manage the Google Home smart speaker, and the Google Assistant app is used to control the digital voice assistant. For users of the HomePod, settings for Siri are specified in the Settings app on a mobile Apple device, and the Home app is used to set up and control smart home devices.

32

Settings

Within each digital voice assistant's companion app is a range of settings that can be used to customize the operation of the related digital voice assistant's device; e.g. the smart speaker containing the digital voice assistant. Some settings include:

Wake word

This is the word that will activate the digital voice assistant on a specific smart speaker device. Different devices have their own range of options for changing the wake word.

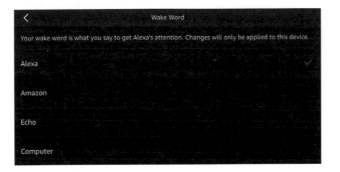

If you have more than one smart speaker device, e.g. several Amazon Echoes in different rooms in your home, separate settings can be applied to each one. For instance, a different wake word can be used for each device.

Location

Each device's location can be specified, and this can then be used by the digital voice assistant to deliver location-specific information, such as a local weather forecast or nearby restaurants.

Language

This can be used to specify a language (or accent) for the digital voice assistant on a specific device.

...cont'd

Measurement units

This can be used to specify measurement for temperature and distance, which will be used for queries such as, "[Device wake word], what is the temperature in London today?", or "[Device wake word], how far is it to New York?" Measurements can be changed as required; e.g. you may usually want distances in kilometers, but change it to miles if you want to find out the traditional length of the marathon in athletics.

Beware

It can become annoying to get a lot of sounds playing for notifications. Keep the number of sounds to a minimum – the notifications should also appear on the digital voice assistant's app on your smartphone or tablet.

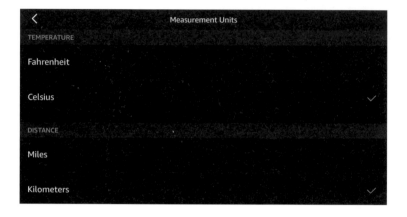

Sounds

This can be used to select device sounds for any alarms that have been set; e.g. "[Device wake word], set a timer for 10 minutes", or for any notification on the devices, such as a calendar event or a message that is received. For alarms, the volume of the alarm can be set and also whether it is an ascending alarm; i.e. it gets louder the longer that it is on.

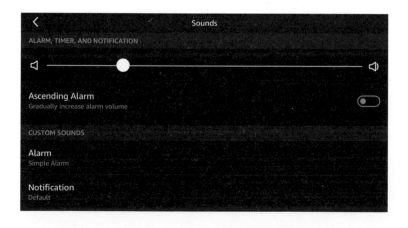

3 Alexa and the Amazon Echo

This chapter looks at one of the most popular digital voice assistants, Amazon's Alexa, and its related smart speaker, the Echo. It shows how to set it up and use it with the Alexa app.

Don't forget

Since Alexa is linked to Amazon's huge range of goods and services, it is a very effective and versatile option for a digital voice assistant.

Don't forget

The standard Echo and the Echo Dot have buttons on the top of the device to control the volume, although this can also be done with voice commands to Alexa.

About Alexa and the Echo

One of the leading digital voice assistants comes from Amazon, in the form of Alexa with the Echo smart speaker.

The Amazon Echo is a hands-free speaker that you use to communicate with Alexa, and this is where content is delivered. Think of the Echo as the body of your digital personal assistant, and Alexa as the brains of the operation. Alexa can react to different voices, and some of the uses for the Echo and Alexa include:

- Playing music from your own music library or through an online radio station.

- Requesting the latest news and sports headlines.

- Setting up processes so that several actions can be performed in sequence.

- Making calls and sending messages to your contacts.

- Controlling smart devices in the home, including lighting systems, central heating and plugs.

The services and information delivered through the Amazon Echo by Alexa are cloud-based, which means that all of the data is stored in an Amazon computer (server) and then delivered through the Amazon Echo when it is requested. Nothing is physically stored on the Echo; it is merely a delivery system. The Echo works through connecting to your home Wi-Fi network: without Wi-Fi it will not function properly.

Models of Echo

There are several different models of Echo, which provide different functionality. This gives you the flexibility of putting different Echo models in different rooms of your home, to create the ultimate Echo experience. The models of the Echo include:

- **Echo.** Now in its second generation, this is the original version of the device, and can be considered as the "standard" Echo. It is a high-quality speaker that provides excellent sound for music, in addition to the full range of services from Alexa. It comes in a range of colors, and fabric covers can also be placed over the device so that it can blend in to any room in your home. The cover style can be selected when you buy the Echo from Amazon.

- **Echo Dot**. This is a smaller version of the standard Echo device and is a good option if you want to expand your Echo system so that you have several devices, in different rooms. If you choose to do this, each Echo can be used independently; e.g. you can play different music in the family room and a bedroom, using a family plan from a compatible service such as Amazon Music.

The Echo Dot and the Echo Spot do not have as powerful speakers as the other Echo models, although external ones can be added with a cable or Bluetooth.

- **Echo Spot**. This is an Echo device that includes a circular screen, like a slightly expanded version of the Echo Dot. It provides the standard information from Alexa and it can also be used to make video calls and display movies or TV shows from a streaming service such as Amazon Video or Netflix.

- **Echo Show**. This is a model of the Echo that comes with a larger screen than the Spot: 7 inches (measured diagonally). It can be used for all of the same functions as the standard Echo, plus it can be used to stream movies and TV shows and make video calls.

- **Echo Plus**. This is the largest Echo model and contains a built-in smart home hub, so it is an excellent option if you want to use it to control other Echo devices and also smart devices in the home (although much of this can also be done with the standard Echo).

Setting up the Echo

The Amazon Echo has to be set up for use through the Alexa app, using an Amazon account. Once this has been done you can begin exploring and using the full functionality of the Amazon Echo and Alexa.

38

1 Download the Amazon Alexa app to your smartphone or tablet

2 Plug in the Amazon Echo. Alexa will tell you when it is ready to be set up, via the Alexa app

3 In the Alexa app, enter your Amazon account username and password and tap on the **Sign In** button. If you do not have an Amazon account, tap on the **Create a New Amazon Account** button

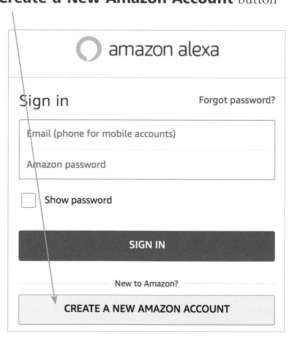

4 Tap on the **Continue** button

Tap on the **Menu** button

Tap on the **Settings** button Settings

Tap on the **Set Up A New Device** button

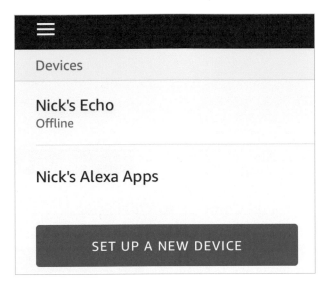

Devices

Nick's Echo
Offline

Nick's Alexa Apps

SET UP A NEW DEVICE

Tap on the required device to set up. This is also the process that is used if you want to set up additional Echo devices after the initial one has been added

Choose a device to set up

By proceeding, you agree to the terms found here.

Echo

Echo Dot

Echo Plus

Don't forget

Several Echo devices linked to the same Amazon account can be used throughout the home so that you can access Alexa in each room, if desired.

...cont'd

 Select a language for Alexa's voice and tap on the **Continue** button

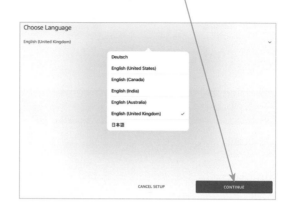

40

 Since Alexa is a cloud-based service, it needs access to the internet via your home Wi-Fi network. Tap on the **Connect To Wi-Fi** button

CONNECT TO WI-FI

 When the light ring on the top of the Echo turns orange, tap on the **Continue** button

CONTINUE

12 In your smartphone's or tablet's Wi-Fi settings, select the **Amazon** network

Wi-Fi	
Wi-Fi	⬤
✓ PlusnetWireless792287	🔒 🤖 ⓘ
PERSONAL HOTSPOTS	
Nick's iPhone 8	▪▪▪ 3G 🔋
CHOOSE A NETWORK...	
Amazon-6DW	🤖 ⓘ

13 Alexa will inform you that you have connected your Wi-Fi to the Echo and ask you to complete the setup process in the Alexa app. Tap on the **Continue** button

Connected to Echo

CONTINUE

14 Tap on your home Wi-Fi network to use this with Alexa

Select your Wi-Fi network

PlusnetWireless792287

•••••••••   SHOW

☐ Save password to Amazon
  Helps connect other devices. Learn More

Don't forget

Each device that is added needs to go through the same setup process as for the initial device.

41

15 Enter your password for the Wi-Fi router

16 Tap on the **Connect** button   CONNECT

17 The Echo is prepared for use. When the **All done!** screen is displayed, the Go To Home button appears at the bottom

All done!

18 Tap on the **Go To Home** button to go to the Homepage of the Alexa app   GO TO HOME

Using the Alexa App

The Alexa app can be used to customize the functionality of Alexa, and change a range of settings.

Changing the wake word

By default, the wake word for the Alexa is "Alexa". This is what is needed to be said before the device will become active and responsive to your commands. However, this can be changed in the Alexa app. To do this:

Hot tip

The Echo name can be changed by selecting **Alexa app** > **Menu** > **Settings** > **Device name** > **Edit,** tapping on the existing name and entering a new one.

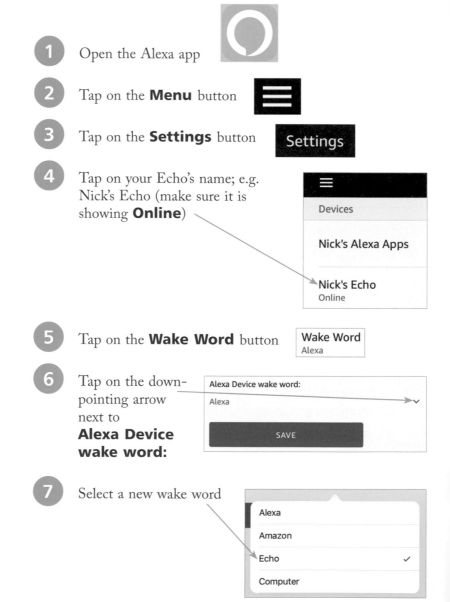

1 Open the Alexa app

2 Tap on the **Menu** button

3 Tap on the **Settings** button

Settings

4 Tap on your Echo's name; e.g. Nick's Echo (make sure it is showing **Online**)

≡

Devices

Nick's Alexa Apps

Nick's Echo
Online

5 Tap on the **Wake Word** button

Wake Word
Alexa

6 Tap on the down-pointing arrow next to **Alexa Device wake word:**

Alexa Device wake word:

Alexa ⌄

SAVE

7 Select a new wake word

Alexa

Amazon

Echo ✓

Computer

Don't forget

Tap on the **Save** button after Step 7 to apply the new wake word for activating Alexa.

SAVE

...cont'd

Setting your location

It is important that Alexa knows your location (or more accurately, the location of your Amazon Echo) so that specific items can be tailored to it; i.e. when you ask for the current weather, or restaurant recommendations nearby. To set the location of your Echo:

 Open the Alexa app and access **Menu** > **Settings** > **Echo name**, as shown on the previous page

2 Tap on the **Edit** button next to **Device location**

Device location
This location will be used for weather, time zone and other local features.

Edit

If you do not specify a location for your Echo, some of Alexa's functionality will be unavailable.

43

3 Enter a location for the Amazon Echo and tap on the **Save** button

Device location
This location will be used for weather, time zone and other local features.

| United Kingdom |

EH1 1AB

Edinburgh

21 High Street

Apartment, suite, unit, building, floor, etc.

State/Province/Region

SAVE

4 The location entered in Step 3 is displayed under the **Device location** heading, and this will be used by Alexa

---

Device location
This location will be used for weather, time zone and other local features.

21 High Street, Edinburgh, GB EH1 1AB

...cont'd

Other settings

Within the Alexa app are the general settings that can be accessed from the Settings button, as with the wake word and location on pages 42-43. In addition, there are a range of options that can be applied for specific functionality for Alexa.

1 Open the Alexa app

2 Tap on the **Menu** button

3 The available categories are listed in the left-hand panel

Music & Books

Lists

Reminders & Alarms

Contacts

Alexa Devices

Routines

Smart Home

Skills & Games

Settings

Things to Try

Help & Feedback

Hot tip

Smart home devices such as lighting, heating and smart plugs can be controlled via the Alexa app, in addition to controlling them through their own dedicated apps that can be downloaded to your smartphone or tablet.

44

4 Tap on one of the categories to view its options and settings

Alexa App Homepage

Once Alexa has been set up, the Homepage can be used to display the requests that have been made of Alexa, and also give feedback about the accuracy of voice commands that have been made.

1 Open the Alexa app and tap on this icon at the bottom of the screen to view the Homepage

2 The top panel offers suggestions for questions to ask Alexa

3 The results for voice commands that have been made are shown below the top panel, with the most recent one at the top

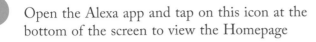

Don't forget

As requests are made of Alexa, the latest one replaces the one before it at the top of the Homepage.

4 Tap on the **More** button next to an item on the Homepage to provide voice feedback

> **Weather in Perth, United Kingdom**
> AccuWeather.com
>
> ☀ 5°
>
> Friday, February 9, 2018
> Partly sunny
>
> Hi 5° / Lo -2°   RealFeel: 0°
> Wind: WNW 18.5 km/h   Precipitation: 7%
>
> Sat   Sun   Mon   Tue   Wed
> Feb 10   Feb 11   Feb 12   Feb 13   Feb 14
> 7°/-1°   4°/-2°   5°/0°   4°/-2°   5°/-1°
>
> More ⌄

Hot tip

Always speak as clearly as possible to Alexa, to give it the best chance of understanding you.

5 Tap on the **Yes** or **No** buttons to provide feedback about whether Alexa heard your command correctly. This is used to train Alexa for subsequent requests

> **Voice feedback**
>
> ▶ *Alexa heard: "alexa what's the weather"*
>
> Did Alexa hear you correctly?
>
> Yes   No

Alexa Skills

The functionality of Alexa, i.e. the tasks that it can perform, is known as "skills". This is similar to using an app on a smartphone or a tablet. Some skills are already pre-installed for Alexa, while others can be added to increase Alexa's functionality. For instance, providing the time and date is a pre-installed skill, while managing a calendar is a skill that can be added. To add more skills for use with Alexa:

Hot tip

Alexa takes requests literally, so if you say, "Alexa, play Wind", the result may be a song of that title from Amazon Music. For a specific item say, "Alexa, ask [skill name] to play Wind".

1 Open the Alexa app and tap on the **Menu** button

2 Tap on the **Skills & Games** button

Skills & Games

3 The Skills Homepage is where you can view available skills and then download them for use with Alexa

4 Tap on a skill in the main skills window, or search for one using the **Categories** button or the **Search all skills** box at the top of the window

CATEGORIES

Search all skills

5 For the selected skill, tap on the **Enable** button, above a description of the skill

Tap on the **All Skills** button in the **Your Skills** section to view all of the skills that you have added.

6 The skill is added to the Skills window, under the **Recently Added** and **All Skills** tabs in the **Your Skills** section. The number of currently-enabled skills is also displayed

 Your Skills

7 To disable a skill, access the **Your Skills** window, select a skill and tap on the **Disable Skill** button. Once a skill has been disabled it can be enabled again, using the same process that was used to enable it initially

DISABLE SKILL

Some pre-installed skills cannot be disabled, e.g. the time and date, and these do not appear in the list of skills.

Music on the Echo

The standard Echo and the Echo Plus are high-quality speakers and so are ideal for playing music around the home. There are several options for this:

- Buy specific tracks or albums of music from Amazon and play them from your Amazon Music library. (Music that is obtained this way can also be played on a range of devices, including PC, Mac, smartphone and tablet – iOS and Android.)

- Subscribe to Amazon Music Unlimited to gain access to over 40 million songs that can be streamed to your Echo.

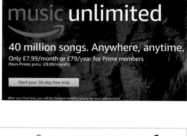

- Join Amazon Prime, which, among a range of other services, offers over two million music tracks for streaming.

Don't forget

In addition to access to Prime Music, Amazon Prime membership also offers unlimited, free one-day delivery on qualifying products; access to movies and TV shows on Prime Video; access to Amazon Pantry for buying everyday household items; and access to Prime Reading for borrowing a wide range of reading material. Amazon Prime is a subscription service that can be paid for monthly or annually.

Prime Music is included with your Prime membership

- Link to another music subscription service such as Spotify (see next page for details).

- Listen to radio stations, using the TuneIn radio service.

- It is also possible to stream music from an Echo to a connected device; i.e. a Bluetooth speaker.

When playing music, Alexa can perform a range of tasks, such as:

- "Alexa, play [album] by [artist]."

- "Alexa, play next/previous song." (If an album is being played.)

- "Alexa, play [song name] by [artist]."

- "Alexa, pause/stop song."

- "Alexa, play songs with Rain in the title."

...cont'd

Subscribing to a streaming service

In addition to using music directly from the Amazon website, it is also possible to connect to music streaming services through the Alexa app:

1 Open the Alexa app and access **Menu** > **Settings**

2 Tap on the **Music & Media** button

3 The current music services are listed

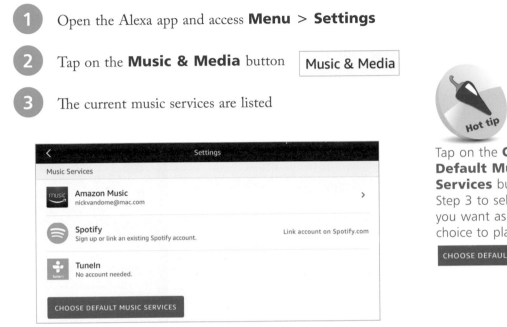

Tap on the **Choose Default Music Services** button in Step 3 to select the one you want as the first choice to play music.

CHOOSE DEFAULT MUSIC SERVICES

49

4 Tap on an item to sign up for the streaming service, or link to it if you already have an account with the service, such as Spotify

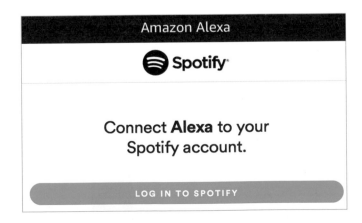

Dropping in with Alexa

Within the home, the Echo is an excellent option for creating an internal intercom system. It is possible to communicate between Echoes in different rooms in the home, and also from the Alexa app to an Echo. This means that you can use your smartphone to communicate with a specific Echo device in the home. This is known as Drop In. To use this:

Hot tip

Voice calls can also be made from Alexa to a smartphone outside the home. To do this, access the Amazon Alexa option in your smartphone's Settings, and enable the Contacts option so that Alexa can use the contacts on your smartphone. Once this has been set up, say, "Alexa, call [recipient's name]" to make a call to their smartphone. This is done using Wi-Fi, so does not need a data connection.

50

1 On your smartphone, open the Alexa app and access **Menu > Settings** and tap on the **Echo** name

Nick's Echo
Online

2 Tap on the **Drop In** button (this can also be done when you first open the Alexa app on your smartphone, by tapping on the **Enable** button in the **Enable Drop In** window)

Drop In
Off

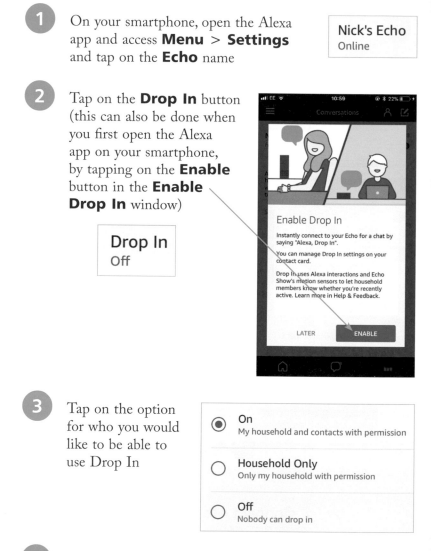

Enable Drop In

Instantly connect to your Echo for a chat by saying "Alexa, Drop In".

You can manage Drop In settings on your contact card.

Drop In uses Alexa interactions and Echo Show's motion sensors to let household members know whether you're recently active. Learn more in Help & Feedback.

LATER   ENABLE

3 Tap on the option for who you would like to be able to use Drop In

⦿ **On**
My household and contacts with permission

○ **Household Only**
Only my household with permission

○ **Off**
Nobody can drop in

4 Tap on this icon on the bottom toolbar of the Alexa app

5 Tap on this icon to add contacts for using Drop In

6 For the selected contact (including yourself, so that you can Drop In on the Echoes within the home) drag the **Allow Drop In** button to On

Nick Vandome
My Profile

Mobile

PERMISSIONS ⑦

Allow Drop In
Contact can Drop In on my Echo Devices

Messages can also be sent to Alexa, in which case the conversation icon in the Alexa app has a green dot on it.

7 Tap on the **OK** button to confirm access to Drop In

Enable Drop In?

When Drop In is enabled, you and your household members can instantly connect to your Echo devices for a video or voice conversation. Interactions with Alexa, and motion sensors on Echo Show, will be used to show a recently active indicator that lets household members know whether you're available.

OK

CANCEL

8 Tap on the button in Step 4 and tap on the **Drop In On [Echo's name]**

≡ Calling & Messaging
DROP IN ON NICK'S ECHO

9 Once the connection is made, you can communicate with the Echo in the same way as making a phone call. Drop in can also be used between Echo devices by saying, **"Alexa, drop in on [Echo name]"**, which is a great way to communicate between Echo devices

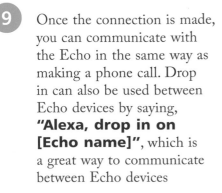
Nick's Echo

Using Smart Home Devices

Smart home devices can be controlled by their own companion app on a smartphone or tablet. Although this works perfectly well, being able to control smart home devices via a digital voice assistant enables the ultimate hands-free flexibility. For Alexa, skills can be added for smart home devices so that voice commands for these items can be actioned. To do this:

Don't forget

Most smart home devices will work with Alexa, but check with the technical specifications of the device to confirm this.

1   Open the Alexa app and access **Menu** > **Smart Home**

Smart Home

2   Tap on the **Your Smart Home Skills** button

YOUR SMART HOME SKILLS

3   Tap on the **Enable Smart Home Skills** button

ENABLE SMART HOME SKILLS

4   Tap on the required skill to add it to Alexa. This will act as a companion to the related smart home device. Without it, Alexa will not be able to communicate with the smart device

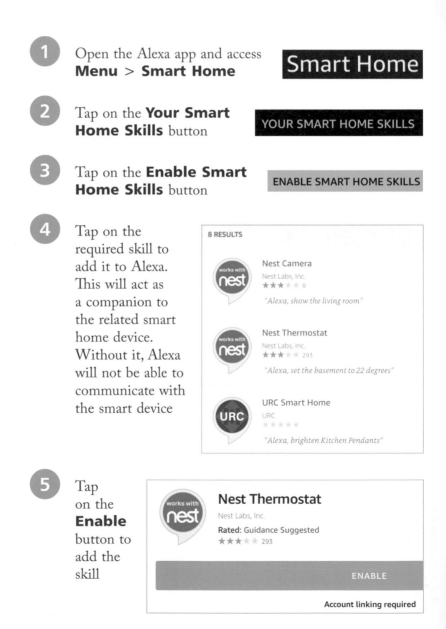

8 RESULTS

Nest Camera
Nest Labs, Inc.
★★★★★ 9
"Alexa, show the living room"

Nest Thermostat
Nest Labs, Inc.
★★★★★ 293
"Alexa, set the basement to 22 degrees"

URC Smart Home
URC
★★★★★
"Alexa, brighten Kitchen Pendants"

5   Tap on the **Enable** button to add the skill

Nest Thermostat
Nest Labs, Inc.
Rated: Guidance Suggested
★★★★★ 293

ENABLE

Account linking required

4 Google Assistant and Google Home

This chapter shows how to use the Google Assistant digital voice assistant and the Google Home smart speaker. It covers setting them up and explains how to use the Google Assistant for a range of tasks.

About Google Assistant and Home

Google Home is Google's smart speaker, which uses the Google Assistant as its digital voice assistant. The Google Home comes in three main models:

The Google Assistant is activated with the wake words, "OK Google", or "Hey Google".

- **The standard Google Home**. This is a high-quality smart speaker that provides excellent sound quality and full access to all of the Google Assistant functionality. It has four colored lights on the top of the device that display different patterns, depending on what the Google Home is doing. It comes with a textured base that is available in four colors.

Google Home and Google Assistant work with the companion Google Home app that can be downloaded to smartphones and tablets from the Google Play Store and the Apple App Store. Google Assistant can be accessed equally well from an Apple mobile device or an Android mobile device, for setting up the Google Home and also for a variety of management tasks.

- **The Google Home Mini**. This offers the same Google Assistant functionality as the standard Google Home, but has a less powerful speaker and is smaller in size. It

has four colored lights on the top of the device which change state depending on the task being performed.

- **The Google Home Max**. This is designed as a high-quality music system and is an excellent option for music fans who also want to have the Google Assistant functionality.

Setting Up

To set up the Google Home smart speaker and the Google Assistant digital voice assistant:

 Download the Google Home app to your smartphone or tablet

 Plug in the Google Home smart speaker. Google Home will tell you when it is ready to be set up, via the Google Home app

3 Open the Google Home app. It will search for any available compatible devices and display any that it finds. Tap on the **Set Up** button

SET UP

📇 Device setup   ⋮

1 device found

GoogleHome9466 is ready for set up   📇

SET UP

---

4 A sound will be emitted by the Google Home smart speaker. Tap on the **Yes** button when you hear it

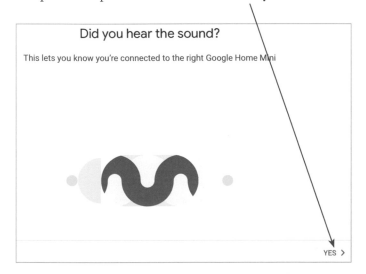

Did you hear the sound?

This lets you know you're connected to the right Google Home Mini

YES ›

A Google Account is needed to use the Google Home app and set up a Google Home speaker. If you do not have one, you can create one when you first start using the app.

When any sound is made from the Google Home, the lights on the top light up.

...cont'd

If you select to share information from your Google Home, Google will have a greater amount of data relating to the device and your use of it. However, this option can also make it work more efficiently.

If you only have one Google Home, it is not necessary to specify a location for it. However, it can be useful for identifying different devices if you have several of them around the home.

5 Select whether you want your Google Home to send information to Google, using either the **Yes, I'm In** button or the **No Thanks** button

6 Select the location within your home of the Google Home and tap on the **Next** button

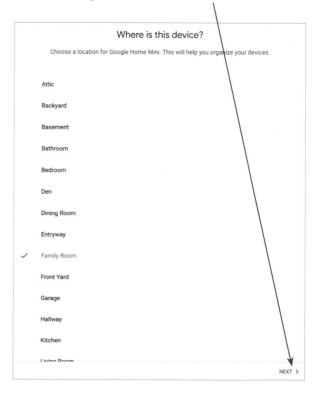

7 Select the Wi-Fi network that will be used by the Google Home and tap on the **Next** button

> × ⋮
>
> ## Choose your Wi-Fi network
>
> Which Wi-Fi network would you like to use to set up your Google Home Mini?
>
> PlusnetWireless792287
>
> juicyanno
>
> SKY0B9E5
>
> VM997653-2G
>
> VM997653-5G
>
> Other Wi-Fi network...
>
> CANCEL   NEXT >

8 Enter the password for the selected Wi-Fi network to be used by the Google Home and tap on the **Connect** button

> ## Enter Wi-Fi Password
>
> PlusnetWireless792287
>
> Password
> ●●●●●●●●●   👁
>
> ☑ Use this Wi-Fi network to set up future devices
>
>   CONNECT >

9 Information about how Google uses information from Google Assistant is displayed. Tap on the arrows next to the options to view them and tap on the **Next** button

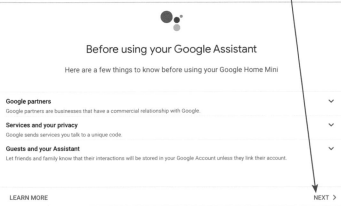

> ## Before using your Google Assistant
>
> Here are a few things to know before using your Google Home Mini
>
> **Google partners**   ⌄
> Google partners are businesses that have a commercial relationship with Google.
>
> **Services and your privacy**   ⌄
> Google sends services you talk to a unique code.
>
> **Guests and your Assistant**   ⌄
> Let friends and family know that their interactions will be stored in your Google Account unless they link their account.
>
> LEARN MORE   NEXT >

57

Hot tip

Read the options in Step 9 to ensure that you are clear about how information gathered from the Google Assistant is used.

...cont'd

Hot tip

The Google Assistant does not need to be trained to recognize voices, and it will work perfectly well without it. However, it can make its performance more efficient, and it is also possible for different users to enable Google Assistant to recognize their voice. This is done in the **Voice Match** section of the Google Home settings.

10 You can teach Google Assistant to recognize your own voice. Tap on the **I Agree** button to set this up

I AGREE ❯

Teach your Assistant to recognize your voice

Voice Match helps your Assistant identify your voice and tell you apart from others by creating a unique model of your voice on this device.

Why set up Voice Match? It allows multiple users to enroll on this device. You can also use your voice to access personal results, which you can turn on after setting up Voice Match.

Keep in mind: A similar voice or recording might be able to access your personal results, too. You can remove Voice Match permission later by turning it off in Assistant settings.

NO THANKS   I AGREE ❯

11 Allow Google Home to access the microphone on your smartphone or tablet, by tapping on the **OK** button

"Google Home" Would Like to Access the Microphone
To record your voice, let Google Home access your microphone.

Don't Allow	OK

12 Repeat the requested phrases and tap on the **Next** button at the end of the process to set up voice recognition

Teach your Assistant to recognize your voice

✓   Complete

✓   Complete

❯   Say "**Hey** Google"

•

13 Tap on an option for the Google Assistant's voice. Tap on the **Play sample** button to preview each example and tap on the **Next** button

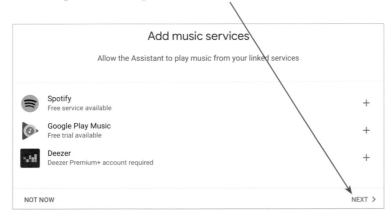

Choose your Assistant's voice

Choose the voice your Assistant will use to talk to you. You can hear a sample of each voice.

✓ Voice 1   ⓟ Play sample

Voice 2   ⓟ Play sample

Voice 3   ⓟ Play sample

Voice 4   ⓟ Play sample

NEXT >

Both female and male voices can be selected as the voice for the Google Assistant.

14 Tap on the **Allow** button to enable Google Home to know its location

Allow "Google Home" to access your location while you are using the app?

Google Home needs to know its location to answer questions related to weather, commute times, etc.

Don't Allow	Allow

Music services on the Google Assistant are subscription services that stream music to the Google Home smart speaker. However, even if a music service has not been added it is possible to listen to numerous free radio stations. Simply ask the Google Assistant for the radio station you would like to listen to.

15 Select a music service to use with the Google Assistant, if required, and tap on the **Next** button

Add music services

Allow the Assistant to play music from your linked services

🟢 **Spotify**
Free service available   +

▶ **Google Play Music**
Free trial available   +

Deezer
Deezer Premium+ account required   +

NOT NOW   NEXT >

...cont'd

Hot tip

Tap on the **Add a payment method** option in Step 16 to add credit or debit card details for your Google Account. This can then be used with the Google Assistant to buy and download content from the Google Play Store, such as music, movies and TV shows.

16 Details of items that have been completed during the setup process are displayed under the **Completed** heading. There are also additional items, under the **Optional** heading, that can be completed at this point, or left to a later time. To add them during the setup process, tap on one of them and follow the wizard

17 Tap on the **Next** button

18 Once the setup process has been completed, tap on the **Continue** button to start using the Google Home smart speaker and the Google Assistant

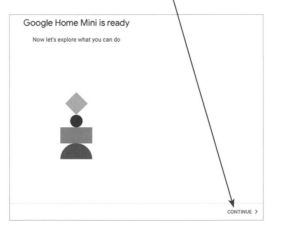

Around the Homepage

The Google Home app can be used to apply a range of settings for how the Google Home smart speaker and the Google Assistant operate. Once you have set these up, the app's Homepage can be used to view the available options:

 Open the Google Home app and tap on the **Discover** button on the bottom toolbar

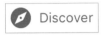

2 The Homepage displays a range of options for using the Google Assistant

3 Tap on the icon on one of the tiles to view options for that item

One of the options for the Google Assistant is to remember important information. However, do not use this to remember sensitive information such as PIN numbers for credit or debit cards, or passwords for unlocking computers, smartphones or tablets, or for websites that may contain financial details. Although the information stored by Google Assistant is secure, it still means that details could become available in the public domain.

...cont'd

Hot tip

One of the most popular uses for the Google Assistant is for getting news updates. The News tile on the Google Home app Homepage can be used to specify which news services are used, and the order in which they deliver the news. Access the page in Step 4 and tap on the cross next to an item to remove it from your news feed. Tap on the **Change Order** button at the top of the window and drag this button to change the order in which news services are delivered.

4 Options for each item are displayed, specific to their own function. This includes items such as news services, traffic updates, and people in your contacts list

✕	News	⋯

Your Assistant will play the news from these sources when you say "listen to the news" or add news to a routine.

Your news sources   CHANGE ORDER

	NPR News Now General	✕
	USA TODAY 5 Things General	✕
S	theScore eSports Sports	✕
	BBC Minute World	✕

5 Tap on this button on one of the tiles and tap on the **Dismiss** button to remove a tile from the Homepage

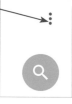

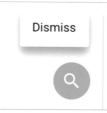

Dismiss

6 Tap on the Menu button in the top left-hand corner of the Homepage to view the Google Assistant menu options

•: Google Assistant

Start with "Ok Google"

To get your Assistant's attention you can say "Ok Google"

7 The Google Home app menu contains a range of options and settings that can be used to customize how the Google Home and the Google Assistant operate. These include adding music streaming services and setting up smart home devices

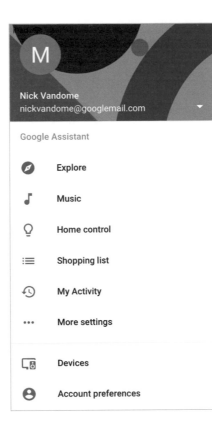

Nick Vandome
nickvandome@googlemail.com

Google Assistant

Explore

Music

Home control

Shopping list

My Activity

More settings

Devices

Account preferences

Hot tip

Tap on the **Home control** option on the Google Home app menu to start adding smart home devices. See pages 76-77 for details.

8 Swipe up the Google Home app Homepage to view more options

Device Settings

Settings for specific Google Home devices can be accessed through the Google Home app. Individual settings can be applied for different Google Home devices in this way. To do this:

 Open the Google Home app and tap on this button in the top right-hand corner of the Homepage

 Any available Google Home devices are displayed

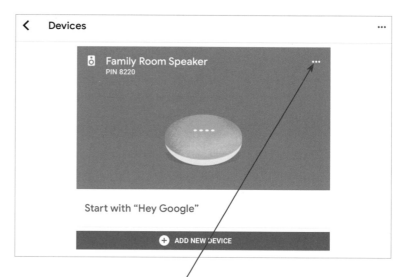

< Devices ...

Family Room Speaker
PIN 8220
...

Start with "Hey Google"

⊕ ADD NEW DEVICE

 Tap on the Menu button in the top right-hand corner and tap on the **Settings** button to access the settings for a specific Google Home device

•••

Settings

Guest mode

Reboot

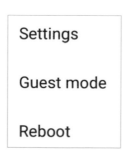
Don't forget

Tap on the **Add New Device** button in Step 2 to add another Google Home smart speaker and set it up with its own specific settings.

4 Use the **General settings** to specify a linked account for the Google Home, select a room for it, add it to a group of devices if required, and manage the Wi-Fi settings for the Google Home

< Device settings
General settings
Linked account(s)
nickvandome@googlemail.com
Name
Family Room Speaker
Group
None added
Wi-Fi
PlusnetWireless792287

5 Use the **Google Assistant settings** to add a music streaming service, add smart home devices, create a shopping list for items to buy from Google, train Google Assistant to recognize specific voices with **Voice Match**, and select settings for a range of items such as news services and calendars with the **More** option (see page 67 for details)

Google Assistant settings
Music
Home control
Shopping list
Voice Match
More
News, My Day, Services...

Don't forget

Voice Match is the same process for recognizing voices as in the original setup process for the Google Home, as shown on page 58.

65

6 Use the **Sound settings** to manage the sound on the Google Home, such as using the **Equalizer** to manage the bass and treble in the speaker

Sound settings
Equalizer
Bass, treble
Group delay correction
0 ms

...cont'd

Hot tip

The output from the Google Home smart speaker can be redirected to a wireless Bluetooth speaker, so that you can move this around the home. To do this, the Bluetooth speaker has to be paired with the Google Home smart speaker, using the **Paired Bluetooth devices** option in Step 7. Once this has been done, turn on the Bluetooth speaker and the Google Home smart speaker should redirect its output to it.

Hot tip

Check on the **Lower volume when listening** box in Step 8 so that the Google Home smart speaker will lower the volume of anything that is playing, such as music, when a request is made of it, so that it can hear the request more clearly.

 7 Use the **Device settings** to manage settings for the specific Google Home devices. These include options for choosing a default speaker such as a Bluetooth speaker to use as the output device for the Google Home, setting alarms and timers, specifying times during which the Google Home will not disturb you, and night mode for restricting items during set times

Device settings

Default speaker
Choose a speaker

Default TV
Choose a TV

Alarms & timers
Adjust volume

Night mode
Reduce volume of responses during specified times

Do not disturb

Guest mode
PIN 8220

Accessibility
Start sound off, end sound off

Paired Bluetooth devices
Enable pairing mode

Preview program
Off

8 Swipe up to the bottom of the page to access more options for controlling the Google Home

☐ **Reverse device controls**
Flip LEDs and volume control when changing position or mounting vertically.

☑ **Lower volume when listening**
When talking to the Assistant, the volume on the controlled TV or speaker will reduce so the Assistant can hear you better.

☑ **Let others control your cast media**
Show a notification on all Android devices connected to your Wi-Fi and let them control media casting from Family Room Speaker

☐ **Help improve Google Home Mini**
Automatically share device stats and crash reports with Google to improve everyone's experience

9 Tap on an item to view the options for customizing it

< **Alarms & timers**

Additional settings

Alarm & timer volume

🔊 ——————————————————●——

More Settings

The More option in Step 5 on page 65 can be used to access settings for your Google Account, device settings and settings for a range of services. To access these:

 Tap on the **More** button on the **Device settings** page

> **More**
> News, My Day, Services...

 Tap on one of the **Account** settings to specify items relating to your Google Account

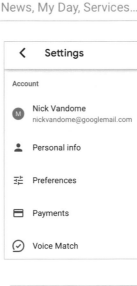

The **More** settings also include options for managing an existing device and also setting up a new one.

Tap on one of the **Services** options to manage these as required. These include selecting music streaming services, setting up smart home devices, selecting news services, creating routines so the Google Assistant can perform a number of tasks in response to a single command, and creating calendar events and appointments

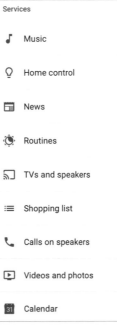

Using and Creating Routines

Routines with the Google Assistant can be used to perform a number of tasks, using a single trigger word or phrase. For instance, you can use routines for different times of the day to provide you with the news, travel conditions, turning lights on or off and activating the heating. All of this is done with a single trigger word or phrase, usually based on the type of routine. To use routines:

Don't forget

The trigger word or phrase for a routine always has to be preceded with "OK Google" or "Hey Google".

 Open the Google Home app, access the Settings section as shown on page 64, and tap on the **More** button

More
News, My Day, Services...

 Tap on the **Routines** button under the **Services** heading

Routines

 The existing, ready-made, routines are displayed

<   **Routines**   ...

Have your Assistant do multiple things with just one command. Use ready-made routines you adjust to fit your day and create custom ones from scratch.

Good morning
5 actions   >

Bedtime
2 actions   >

Leaving home
0 action   >

I'm home
1 action   >

Commuting to work
4 actions   >

Commuting home
2 actions   >

---

4   Tap on a routine to view its details

5 Items that are checked On, with a white tick symbol in a blue box, are the ones that will be activated when the trigger word or phrase is used with Google Assistant

Tap on the **When I say...** option in Step 5 to edit the trigger word or phrase for the routine.

Tap on the **Change Order** button in Step 5 to edit the order in which items are actioned within a routine.

CHANGE ORDER

6 Tap on any action that you want to add to the routine

☑ Adjust media volume

ADD ACTION

And then play...

○ Music

○ News

◉ Radio

7 Tap on the **Save** button to keep any changes that have been made to the routine

SAVE

Beware

It is best not to create too many routines in case you cannot remember the trigger word for them all, or what they do.

...cont'd

Creating custom routines

In addition to using the ready-made routine for the Google Assistant, it is also possible to create your own custom routines. This means that you can specify the actions that are used in the routine and also the trigger word or phrase. To do this:

1 Tap on this button on the Routines Homepage `+`

2 Tap on the **Add a command** button on the **New routines** page to create a custom trigger word or phrase for the new routine

> **<** **New routines**
>
> When I say...
>
> Add a command

3 Tap on this button to create a new trigger word or phrase for the routine `+`

4 Enter the word or phrase to use for the routine, under the **When I say...** heading

> **<** **Add new command**
>
> When I say...
> Relax

5 Tap on the **Save** button to save the new command **SAVE**

6 Tap on the **Back** button on the **Edit commands** page to go back to the New routines page

> **<** **Edit commands**
>
> Relax

7 Tap on the **Add Action** button to specify an action for the Google Assistant to perform when the trigger command is used

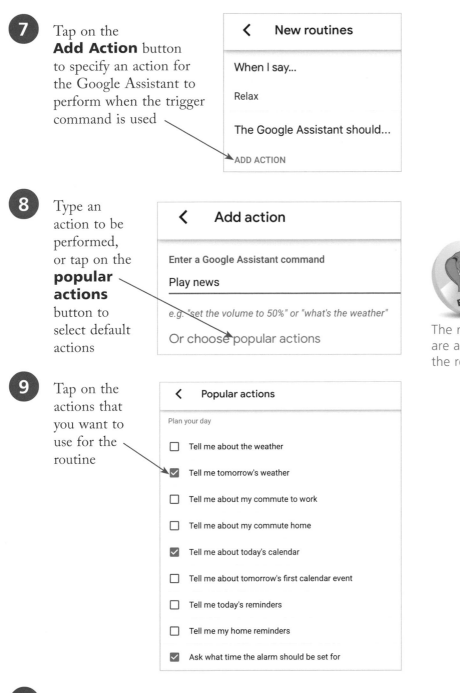

> **<** New routines
>
> When I say...
>
> Relax
>
> The Google Assistant should...
>
> ADD ACTION

8 Type an action to be performed, or tap on the **popular actions** button to select default actions

> **<** Add action
>
> Enter a Google Assistant command
> Play news
>
> *e.g. "set the volume to 50%" or "what's the weather"*
>
> Or choose popular actions

Beware

The more actions that are added, the longer the routine will take.

9 Tap on the actions that you want to use for the routine

> **<** Popular actions
>
> Plan your day
>
> ☐ Tell me about the weather
>
> ☑ Tell me tomorrow's weather
>
> ☐ Tell me about my commute to work
>
> ☐ Tell me about my commute home
>
> ☑ Tell me about today's calendar
>
> ☐ Tell me about tomorrow's first calendar event
>
> ☐ Tell me today's reminders
>
> ☐ Tell me my home reminders
>
> ☑ Ask what time the alarm should be set for

10 Tap on the **Add** button to add the selected actions to the routine

 ADD

...cont'd

 Tap on the **Add Media** button to add media options

And then play...

ADD MEDIA

 Tap on any media items that you want to add to the routine

Hot tip

You do not have to add any media to a routine. If you do not want any, tap on the **Nothing** button at the bottom of the list in Step 12.

<   **Add media**

What media would you like to play?

⦿   Music

○   News

○   Radio

 Tap on the **Add** button   ADD

 The items in the routine, and their order, are listed

<   New routines   SAVE

When I say...

Relax   >

The Google Assistant should...   CHANGE ORDER

✕   Tell me tomorrow's weather

✕   Tell me about today's calendar

✕   Ask what time the alarm should be set for

ADD ACTION

And then play...

⦿   Music   ✿

○   News   ✿

○   Radio   ✿

 Tap on the **Save** button to add a new routine   SAVE

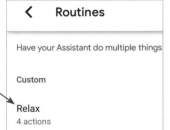 The routine is added on the Routines page, under the **Custom** heading

<   **Routines**

Have your Assistant do multiple things

Custom

Relax
4 actions

Adding Actions

The Google Assistant can perform an extensive range of tasks, without any additions: answering queries, reading the news, providing traffic updates and searching the web, to name a few. However, it is possible to expand the Assistant's functionality through the use of actions. These are similar to using apps on smartphones and tablets: the action enables the Google Assistant to perform tasks specific to the action that has been added.

Viewing actions
There are over a million actions that can be added, and these can be viewed in the Google Home app. To do this:

1 Open the Google Home app and tap on the Menu button in the top left-hand corner of the **Discover** page

2 Tap on the **Explore** button

3 Suggested actions are listed on the **Explore** page

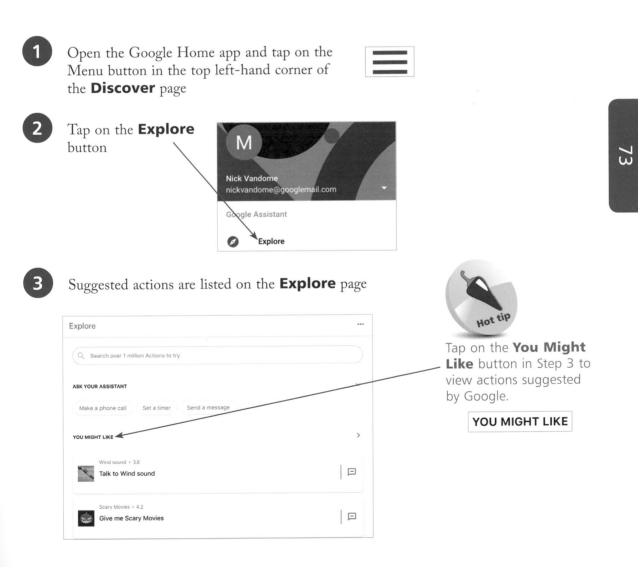

73

Hot tip

Tap on the **You Might Like** button in Step 3 to view actions suggested by Google.

YOU MIGHT LIKE

...cont'd

Don't forget

Actions on the Google Assistant are equivalent to skills on the Amazon Alexa digital voice assistant.

74

 Tap on an item to view its details

Wind sound

HomeApps.ai ★ 3.6

TRY IT

Listen to a strong wind sound

ASK YOUR ASSISTANT

Talk to Wind sound

DETAILS

Music & audio

 Tap on the **Try It** button to activate the action

Wind sound

HomeApps.ai ★ 3.6

TRY IT

 The details page in Step 4 contains the commands that can be used with the Google Assistant to access the functionality of the action

ASK YOUR ASSISTANT

Talk to Wind sound

Searching for actions

There are over a million actions that can be used with the Google Assistant, and they can be searched for using the Google Home app. To do this:

1 Access the **Explore** Homepage, as shown on page 73, and tap in the Search box at the top of the page

2 Enter a topic, or a specific keyword, to view the available actions

3 Tap on one of the actions to view its details

4 Tap on the **Try It** button to make the action available with the Google Assistant

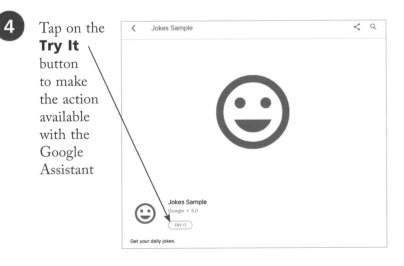

Beware

Always test an action once it has been added, to ensure the process has worked correctly and the Google Assistant can recognize the action.

Linking Smart Home Devices

Smart home devices such as smart lighting and smart heating can be controlled using a Google Home smart speaker and the Google Assistant. Once this has been set up, you can control your compatible smart home devices with a voice command to the Google Assistant, such as, "Okay Google, turn on the kitchen lights", or "Hey Google, set the heating to 20 degrees". To add this functionality:

Don't forget

Smart home devices have to be installed, powered on, and connected to your Wi-Fi network in order for the Google Home app to be able to link to them.

Beware

The action name for a smart home device may not always be exactly the same as the device name. If you cannot find it, try different variations of the name or look on the device's website to see what name is used for it there.

 1 Open the Google Home app and tap on the Menu button in the top left-hand corner of the **Discover** page

2 Tap on the **Home control** button

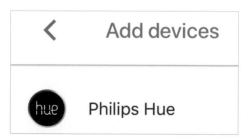

Nick Vandome
nickvandome@googlemail.com

Google Assistant

⊘ Explore

♪ Music

♀ Home control

3 Tap on this button to add a new smart home device

 +

4 Swipe up the page to view all of the available devices. Tap on the one that you want to add

< **Add devices**

hue **Philips Hue**

5 For some devices, there is a requirement to sign-in to the online service for the device. This gives greater functionality. Enter your sign in details or tap on the **Create an account** button to create a new account

Smart home devices can also be linked to the Google Assistant by accessing the relevant skill from the **Explore** button on the menu in Step 2 on the previous page. Locate the skill and tap on the **Link** button to access the option in Step 3 on the previous page and follow the next three steps.

6 Once items have been added, they are available on the **Home control** Homepage, under the **Devices** heading. Devices can then be managed by selecting them here (see page 78)

Smart home devices can also be controlled through their own companion apps on a smartphone or tablet. However, they have to be added to the Google Home app as described here in order to enable them to work with the Google Assistant.

Managing Home Devices

Within the Google Home app there are a limited number of ways for managing smart home devices, such as assigning rooms for them. To do this:

Smart home devices usually have a wider range of management functions from within their own companion apps that can be downloaded to a smartphone or tablet.

1 Tap on a linked device on the **Home control** page

> TP-Link Kasa
>
> My Smart Plug

2 Tap on one of the options to access its settings

> ‹ Device Info
>
> Set a nickname ✏
>
> Room
> Family Room
>
> Name from TP-Link Kasa
> My Smart Plug

3 One of the options is usually for assigning a room for the device. Tap on a room as required

> ‹ Room
>
> My rooms
>
> ○ Bedroom
> ◉ Family Room
> ○ Hall 1
> ○ Hall 2
> ○ Living room

4 Tap on the **Rooms** tab on the **Home control** page to view rooms that have been set up with smart home devices. Tap on a room to view the devices that have been assigned to it

> ‹ Home control ···
>
> DEVICES   ROOMS
>
> **Add your devices to rooms**
> 1 device is not in a room. Adding device in a room enables commands like "turn on the living room lights".
>
> LATER   ASSIGN ROOM
>
> ⌄ Bedroom
>   4 devices   ✏
>
> ⌃ Family Room
>   2 devices   ✏
>
>   My Smart Plug
>
>   Family Room Speaker

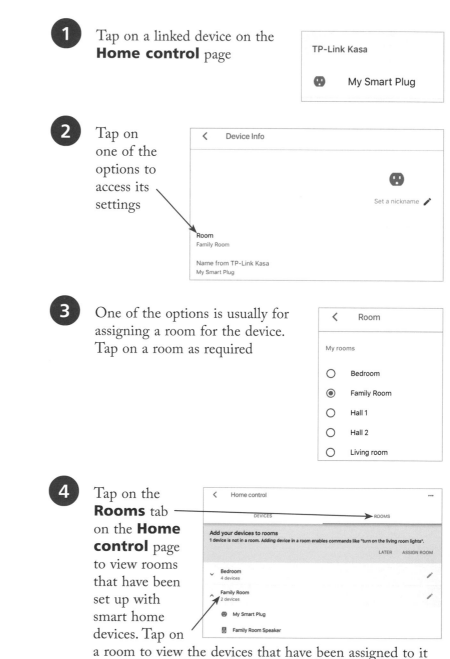

5 HomePod and the Home App

This chapter covers Apple's smart speaker, and the Home app for controlling devices.

About the HomePod

The HomePod is Apple's smart speaker, which uses Siri for voice commands. It is a high-quality speaker that is excellent for listening to music and other audio content. The HomePod is considerably more expensive than the Amazon Echo or the Google Home, but it is a serious option if high-quality music is what you are after.

The HomePod works with the Home app that is pre-installed on Apple's mobile devices, and it uses the digital voice assistant Siri for voice controls.

The HomePod can be set up using an iPhone, an iPad or an iPod Touch, running iOS. To do this:

Beware

Apple mobile devices need to be running iOS 11.2.5, or later, in order to use the HomePod. Also, an iCloud account is required to use the HomePod.

1 Plug in the HomePod and turn on the power

2 Hold the Apple mobile device running iOS next to the HomePod

3 Tap on the **Set Up** button

4 Select a room where the HomePod is located and tap on the **Continue** button

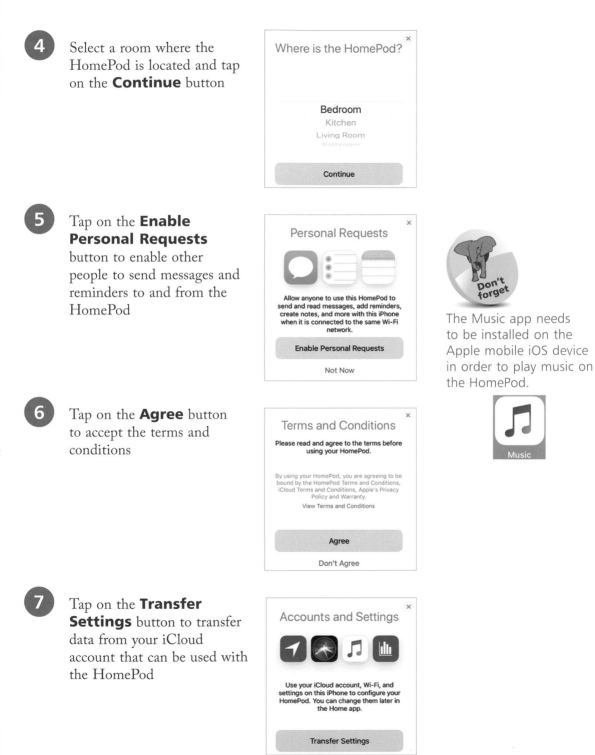

×
Where is the HomePod?

Bedroom
Kitchen
Living Room
Bathroom

Continue

5 Tap on the **Enable Personal Requests** button to enable other people to send messages and reminders to and from the HomePod

×
Personal Requests

Allow anyone to use this HomePod to send and read messages, add reminders, create notes, and more with this iPhone when it is connected to the same Wi-Fi network.

Enable Personal Requests

Not Now

Don't forget

The Music app needs to be installed on the Apple mobile iOS device in order to play music on the HomePod.

Music

6 Tap on the **Agree** button to accept the terms and conditions

×
Terms and Conditions

Please read and agree to the terms before using your HomePod.

By using your HomePod, you are agreeing to be bound by the HomePod Terms and Conditions, iCloud Terms and Conditions, Apple's Privacy Policy and Warranty.
View Terms and Conditions

Agree

Don't Agree

7 Tap on the **Transfer Settings** button to transfer data from your iCloud account that can be used with the HomePod

×
Accounts and Settings

Use your iCloud account, Wi-Fi, and settings on this iPhone to configure your HomePod. You can change them later in the Home app.

Transfer Settings

...cont'd

 Completion of the HomePod setup process is indicated by a green tick in a green circle

 Options for how you can use the HomePod with Siri are displayed. Tap on the **Done** button to finish the setup

 Tap on the **Home** button on the Homepage of the iOS device to view the HomePod on the Home app

Tap on the **Home** button on the bottom toolbar of the Home app to view the HomePod, under the Favorite Accessories heading. Tap on the **HomePod** to view its details and apply a range of settings

Using Siri with the HomePod

Once the HomePod has been set up, Siri can be used with it to perform a range of functions. Some commands to try include:

- "Hey Siri, what's the latest news?"

- "Hey Siri, what's the weather for tomorrow?"

- "Hey Siri, tell me about the traffic for this evening."

- "Hey Siri, what's the square root of 64?"

- "Hey Siri, how much is US$50 in pounds sterling?"

- "Hey Siri, tell me a joke."

- "Hey Siri, turn on the lights in the living room." (If smart lighting is available and has been added to the Home app.)

- "Hey Siri, dim the dining room lights." (If smart lighting is available and has been added to the Home app.)

For more information about using smart home devices with the Home app, see pages 84-94.

- "Hey Siri, turn on the heating." (If smart heating is available and has been added to the Home app.)

- "Hey Siri, turn the temperature in the bedroom to 20 degrees." (If smart heating is available and been added to the Home app.)

- "Hey Siri, tell me the next event on my calendar."

- "Hey Siri, set a timer for 10 minutes."

- "Hey Siri, create a reminder to send Dad a birthday card in two weeks from today."

- "Hey Siri, play the best of Frank Sinatra from my music library." (This is done through the Music app.)

- "Hey Siri, pick some music." Siri will randomly pick some music from your music library.

- "Hey Siri, play a country music radio station."

Using the Home App

On Apple mobile devices using iOS, the Home app can be used to link to smart home devices so that Siri can be used to control them from an iPhone, iPad or iPod Touch. To use the Home app:

1 Tap on the **Home** app on the iPhone's, iPad's or iPod Touch's Homepage

Don't forget

The Home app comes pre-installed with the iOS mobile operating system for iPhones, iPads and iPod Touches.

2 Tap on the **Get Started** button to start adding a smart home device

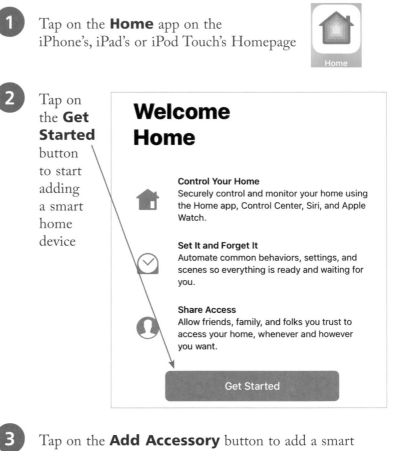

Welcome Home

Control Your Home
Securely control and monitor your home using the Home app, Control Center, Siri, and Apple Watch.

Set It and Forget It
Automate common behaviors, settings, and scenes so everything is ready and waiting for you.

Share Access
Allow friends, family, and folks you trust to access your home, whenever and however you want.

Get Started

Don't forget

Smart home devices that are accessed from Apple iOS mobile devices need to support HomeKit, which is the Apple software framework for smart home devices. Most mainstream smart home devices support the HomeKit framework.

3 Tap on the **Add Accessory** button to add a smart home device to the Home app

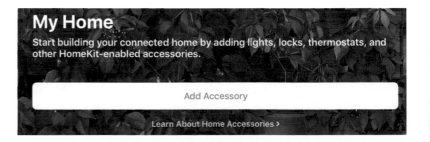

My Home
Start building your connected home by adding lights, locks, thermostats, and other HomeKit-enabled accessories.

Add Accessory

Learn About Home Accessories >

4 The camera on the iPhone, iPad or iPod Touch can be used to identify the code for the device. This is usually an eight-digit code on part of the device; e.g. the hub for a smart lighting system, or the smart thermostat for a smart heating system. Position the camera so that it can see the code, which is done within a white box. The code should them be captured automatically

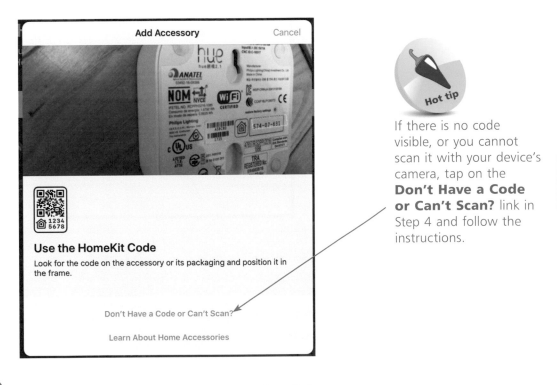

Hot tip

If there is no code visible, or you cannot scan it with your device's camera, tap on the **Don't Have a Code or Can't Scan?** link in Step 4 and follow the instructions.

5 Tap on the required item that has been identified

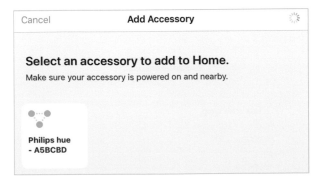

...cont'd

6 Details about each item that are connected to the device are displayed

	1 of 10	Next

Philips hue
- A5BCBD

Identify Accessory

Philips hue - A5BCBD

Room   Default Room

Include in Favorites

Your favorite accessories appear in Control Center and in the Home tab, so you can access them quickly.

Don't forget

Each smart home device has to be added separately to the Home app before it becomes available for use.

7 Tap on the **Next** button   Next

8 For a device such as a smart lighting system, each light bulb that has been installed is listed. Tap on the **Next** button to move through all of the items

‹ Back	3 of 10	Next

Default Room
Hue color la...

Identify Accessory

Hue color lamp

Room   Default Room

...cont'd

9 The final listing for the device is indicated here

**Default Room
Hue white la...**

Identify Accessory

10 Tap on the **Done** button

11 All of the items that have been added for a specific device are displayed on the Home app Homepage

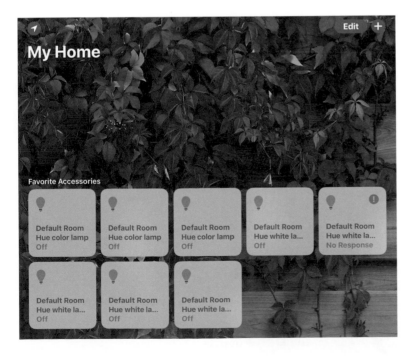

Once items have been added to the Home app they can then be controlled with voice commands on an iPhone, an iPad or an iPod Touch, using Siri.

Managing the Home App

Once devices have been added to the Home app they can be managed within the app. This also enables Siri to control the devices, in response to voice commands. To manage devices:

1 Open the **Home** app and tap on the **Home** button on the bottom toolbar

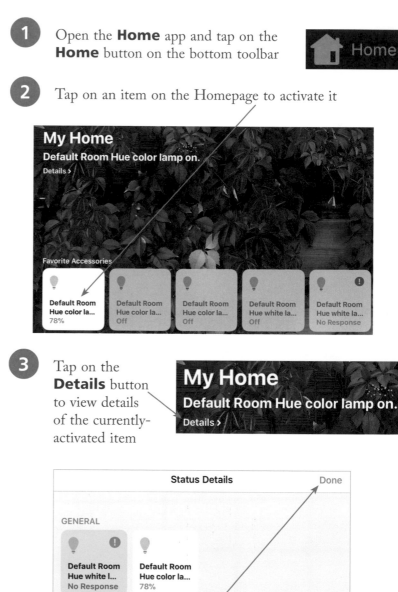

2 Tap on an item on the Homepage to activate it

My Home
Default Room Hue color lamp on.
Details ›

Favorite Accessories

| Default Room Hue color la... 78% | Default Room Hue color la... Off | Default Room Hue color la... Off | Default Room Hue white la... Off | Default Room Hue white la... No Response |

3 Tap on the **Details** button to view details of the currently-activated item

My Home
Default Room Hue color lamp on.
Details ›

Status Details   Done

GENERAL

| Default Room Hue white l... No Response | Default Room Hue color la... 78% |

4 Tap on the **Done** button

Beware

It is important to assign devices to specific rooms, so Siri knows where the items are located and can respond to voice commands accordingly. See pages 92-94 for details.

Editing the Home app

The appearance of the Home app can be customized, and it is also possible to invite other people to have access to the app so that they can control smart devices with it too. To do this:

1 Tap on the **Edit** button in the top right-hand corner of the **Home** page

2 Tap the arrow to the right of **My Home**

3 Tap under the **Name** heading to change the name of the Homepage

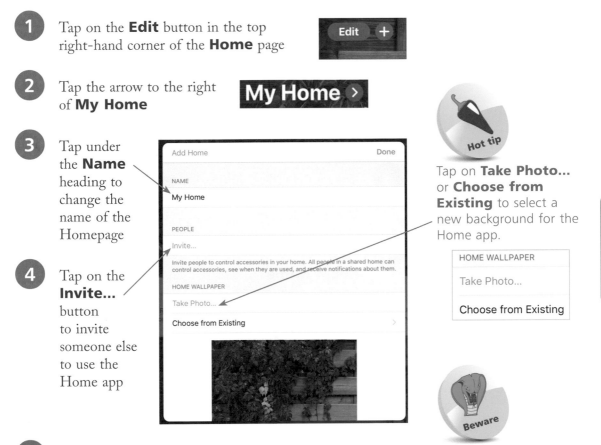

4 Tap on the **Invite...** button to invite someone else to use the Home app

> **Hot tip**
>
> Tap on **Take Photo...** or **Choose from Existing** to select a new background for the Home app.
>
> | HOME WALLPAPER |
> |---|
> | Take Photo... |
> | Choose from Existing |

5 Enter the email address of the person that you want to invite and tap on the **Send Invite** button

Cancel	**Add People**	Send Invite

To: eilidh

Eilidh
other eilidhvandome@googlemail.com

Eilidh
iCloud eilidhvandome1@icloud.com

> **Beware**
>
> Swipe up to get to the bottom of the page in Step 3, and tap on the **Remove Home** button to remove the current home devices. This will remove all of the items that have been added.
>
> | Remove Home |
> |---|

Managing Rooms

The Home app can also be used to assign rooms to specific devices. This can be useful if you have several of the same type of device: once rooms have been assigned for devices, you can instruct Siri accordingly; e.g. "Hey Siri, turn on the smart plug in the living room", or "Hey Siri, turn on the bedroom lights". To assign rooms to specific smart home devices:

Beware

Give rooms common, recognizable names so that if other people are accessing the Home app they will be able to find the rooms easily.

1 Open the **Home** app and tap on the **Rooms** button on the bottom toolbar

2 Tap on the **Edit** button in the top right-hand corner

3 Tap on the right-pointing arrow next to **Default Room**

4 Under the **Room Name** heading, enter a new name for the default room

5 Tap on the **Done** button in the top right-hand corner

6 The room's new name is shown on the **Rooms** Homepage

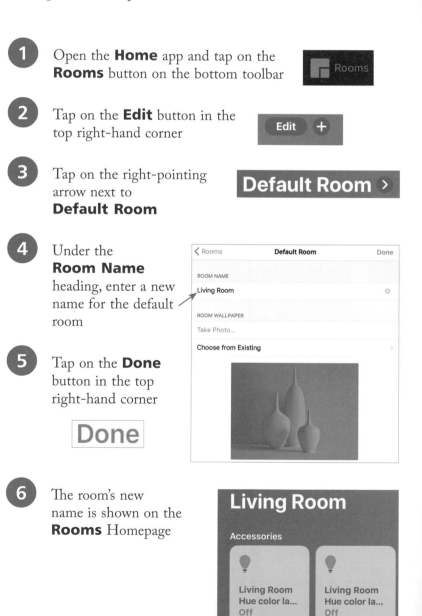

Adding rooms

To add more rooms to the Home app:

 Tap on this button above the current room name

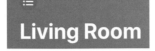

 Tap on the **Add Room** button

Add Room	**Living Room**	Done

ROOM NAME

Living Room

 Enter a name for the new room, under the **Room Name** heading, and tap on the **Save** button

Cancel	**Add Room**	Save

ROOM NAME

Bedroom

ROOM WALLPAPER

Take Photo...

Choose from Existing

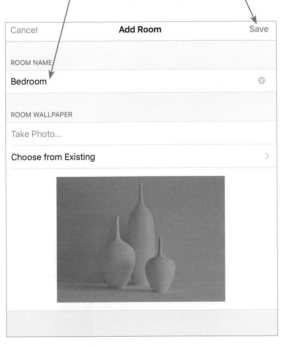

Don't forget

Before a new room is added, the current room name is displayed in Step 2.

...cont'd

 Tap on the **Done** button

< Rooms	**Bedroom**	Done
ROOM NAME		
Bedroom		

5 The new room is displayed in the Rooms section of the Home app. At this point it is empty; i.e. it does not have any devices assigned to it

Hot tip

Swipe left and right on the Rooms Homepage to view the different rooms that have been added.

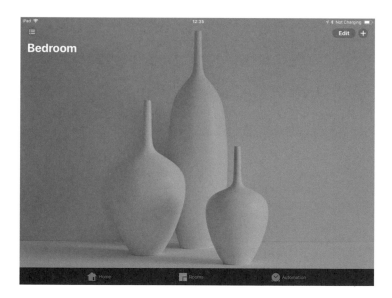

Assigning devices
Once a room has been added, devices can be assigned to it:

1 Tap on the **Home** button on the bottom toolbar

2 Tap on the **Edit** button in the top right-hand corner

3 Tap on one of the devices on the Homepage

4 The device's current location is displayed under the **Room** options. Tap on this to edit the room

Living Room Hue white lamp — Done

Living Room
Hue white la...
Off

Hue white lamp

Room — Living Room

Include in Favorites

Hot tip

Drag the **Include in Favorites** button On in Step 3 to display the device on the **Home** page of the Home app. Drag it off to hide it.

93

5 Tap on a new room to assign it to the device

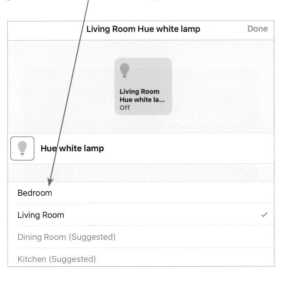

Living Room Hue white lamp — Done

Living Room
Hue white la...
Off

Hue white lamp

Bedroom

Living Room ✓

Dining Room (Suggested)

Kitchen (Suggested)

Beware

Devices do not have to be physically located in the room specified in the Home app. However, if they are in a different location they will be turned on and off according to their location in the app. Try to ensure that the physical location and the location specified in the app are the same.

...cont'd

6 Tap on the **Done** button to assign the selected device to the room and return to the Home app Homepage

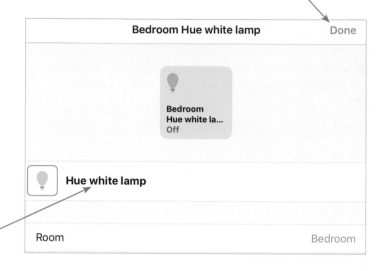

Hot tip

Device names can be edited by tapping on them here and overtyping the current name. This can be useful, as it means they can be given names that are specific to the rooms in which they are located.

7 Tap on the **Done** button in the top right-hand corner of the Home app Homepage to finish assigning the device to the selected room

8 Tap on the **Rooms** button on the bottom toolbar to view devices that have been assigned to specific rooms

6 Using Smart Devices

This chapter gives an overview of using smart home devices, and apps that can be used with them.

Installing Devices

The operation for smart home devices is generally similar for different types of devices, although some require extra hardware for them to operate. The general process for setting up a smart device in the home is:

Don't forget

Depending on the type of smart home device, the order of the installation steps may vary slightly.

1 Physically install the device; e.g. fit a smart light bulb into a light fitting, plug a smart plug into a power socket, or install a smart thermostat (this should be done by a recognized tradesman). For some devices, they can be turned on at this initial step

2 Download the relevant app for the smart device; e.g. the Hue app for the Philips Hue smart lighting system, the TP-LINK Kasa app for the smart TP-LINK plug, and the Nest app for the Nest smart thermostat.

Apps can be downloaded to smartphones or tablets from the Apple App Store (for iOS devices) or the Google Play Store (for Android devices)

3 Install a bridge to your Wi-Fi router. This is only applicable for some smart devices, such as the Philips Hue lighting system. If a bridge is used, it acts as the connection between the smart home device and the router, and provides a greater range of functionality

4 Enable the required skill/action for your digital voice assistant (in a similar way to adding the app to your smartphone or tablet)

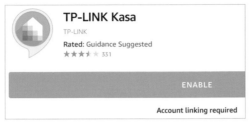

TP-LINK Kasa
TP-LINK
Rated: Guidance Suggested
★★★★★ 331

ENABLE

Account linking required

5 Turn on the smart device (if it has not already been turned on in Step 1)

6 Open the device's app. Initially, you may have to set up an account for the app, using an email address and password. This will enable you to control the device remotely when you are away from home. Tap on the **Create Account** button to create a new account

Email
Password
LOG IN
Forgot password?
Create Account   Skip

7 The device has to be added to the app so that the app can communicate with it and control it. Tap on the add device option to add a new device

≡   Devices   +

No devices yet!
Add your devices by tapping the button on the top right. Your saved devices will be listed here.

Hot tip

Digital voice assistants, and apps for smart devices, have to discover the device so the setup process can be completed. This is usually done by tapping on the **Discover Device** button in the digital voice assistant's app or the smart device's app.

Hot tip

Each new device will have to be added to the app; e.g. if a new smart plug is added to a smart plug system it will have to be added, even if there are already plugs that have been recognized by the app.

...cont'd

The device name will be the one used to give commands to a digital voice assistant; e.g. "Siri, turn on My Smart Plug".

The Wi-Fi network for the smart device will briefly appear in the Wi-Fi Settings on your smartphone or tablet as the connected network. However, when you return to the device's app, the Wi-Fi will revert to your normal home network; e.g. the name of your home router.

8 Select the device that is to be added. For some apps there will only be a single type of device to add; for others there may be several options

Add Device

TP-LINK   WORKS WITH KASA

Choose from pre-configured devices ①

Smart Plug   Smart Plug
Mini or Lite Series

9 Give the device a specific name, or use the default one

Device name

Let's give it a friendlier name, like "Living Room Lamp"

My Smart Plug

NEXT

10 The device has to be linked to your home Wi-Fi network

CHOOSE A NETWORK...

TP-LINK_Smart Plug_0875

(unless it operates using a different means of wireless communication). To do this, go to the Wi-Fi settings on your smartphone or tablet and select the Wi-Fi network specific to the device

11 In the device's app, enter the password for the Wi-Fi router, to enable the device to connect to the home Wi-Fi network. Tap on the **Next** button

Joining your network

Please enter your Wi-Fi password so we can invite your device to join.

Make sure you enter the correct password to prevent failed installation.

🛜 PlusnetWireless792287

••••••••••

☑ Save Password

NEXT

Don't forget

The network password is the one for your home Wi-Fi router. It should be on a sticker on the body of the router.

12 If the installation has been successful, you will be notified of this in the final window. Tap on the **Done** button to complete the installation process

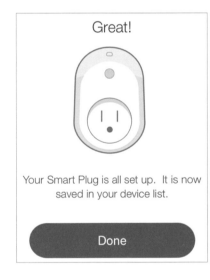

Great!

Your Smart Plug is all set up. It is now saved in your device list.

Done

13 Once the device has been set up, you will then be able to control it through the app, or by using a digital voice assistant. This includes turning it on or off and setting timed schedules for the device

☰ Devices ＋

SMART PLUGS

My Smart Plug ⏻

Related Apps for Devices

Most smart home devices have their own companion apps that can be used to control and manage the devices. Some points to bear in mind about smart home apps:

- The apps usually have the same name as the smart home device; e.g. the Philips Hue smart lighting app is named Philips Hue, the Nest smart heating app is named Nest, etc.

- Apps are used on smartphones and tablets so that you can always have access for controlling your smart home devices.

- Apps can be downloaded from the Apple App Store and the Google Play Store and can be used on most smartphones and tablets to access smart home devices.

- Apps can be used to control smart home devices when you are in the home, and also remotely when you are away from home, or even out of the country.

- Apps can be used to perform standard actions such as turning devices on or off, and they can also perform more complicated tasks, such as creating a routine to apply a number of actions to the device in sequence.

Elements of smart device apps

Each smart device operates slightly differently but they all share similar functionality:

Companion apps can also be used to link to online sites for the smart home device and register on the site. This gives more control for using the device with the companion app.

 One of the main functions of a smart home device app is to turn the devices on and off. Tap on the buttons for this

New scene

YOUR ROOMS

Living room
All lights are on

Hall 1
All lights are off

Hall 2
All lights are on

Bedroom
All lights are off

2 Smart home device apps can also be used to create routines and schedules for turning devices on and off at specific times, or for certain conditions such as the arrival of dusk, or if no one being present in the house. Tap on items within the app to apply them and customize them

Different routines can be created for weekdays and weekends.

Routines	
🏠 Home & Away	>
🌅 Wake up	>
🌙 Go to sleep	>
🕐 Other routines	>
🔔 Timers	>

3 A range of settings can be applied with smart device apps, including for accessing the app at home or remotely. Tap on each setting to view its options

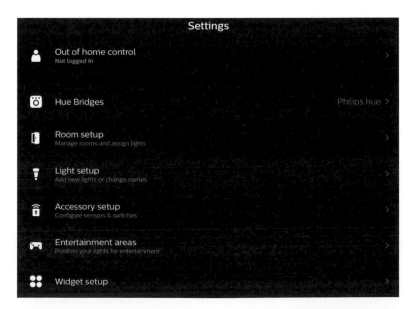

Settings	
👤 Out of home control Not logged in	>
📷 Hue Bridges	Philips hue >
📱 Room setup Manage rooms and assign lights	>
💡 Light setup Add new lights or change names	>
📶 Accessory setup Configure sensors & switches	>
🎮 Entertainment areas Position your lights for entertainment	>
⠿ Widget setup	>

Smart Home Hubs

Once you start adding smart home devices it is easy to see the appeal of them (ease of use, wide range of functionality, and the ability to access them remotely through companion apps), and so it is logical that you will want to add more devices to your smart home ecosystem. As this is done, it can become slightly overwhelming if you have numerous apps on your smartphone or tablet for controlling your devices. This is where a smart home hub comes in: a hub can be used to link all of your smart home devices, regardless of the wireless protocols that they use to communicate with their related apps, and enables you to control them all with one app.

Digital voice assistants and their related smart speakers are examples of smart home hubs; e.g. you can control your smart home devices with voice commands using Amazon Echo, Google Assistant and Apple's Siri. However, you will still need the individual apps for the devices if you want to control them from your smartphone or tablet.

In addition to digital voice assistants, there are also dedicated smart home hubs that are designed specifically for use with a wide range of smart home devices. Some models include:

- Wink Hub.

- Logitech Harmony.

- Samsung SmartThings Hub.

Some issues to consider when buying a smart home hub:

- Does the hub support voice control? Most of them do, but there are some that do not. This is likely to change, as voice control becomes more of a requirement for users, but check the device's specification to make sure this is included.

- Does the hub support all of the major wireless protocols for smart home devices; i.e. Wi-Fi, Bluetooth, 3/4G, Zigbee and Z-Wave?

- Does the hub support the major mobile operating systems? They will all support iOS for Apple devices and Android for Android devices, but if you have a mobile device that uses a different type of operating system, check the specifications.

Don't forget

If you already have a digital voice assistant there is no real need to get a separate smart home hub, unless you want to control all of your devices from a single app.

Using a smart home hub

Smart home hubs use their own companion apps to link to the hub, and smart home devices can then be controlled and managed through the app. To use a smart home hub:

1 Install the smart home hub and power it On

Smart home hubs should be able to identify and connect to all of your smart home devices.

2 Download the related app from the Apple App Store or the Google Play Store

Wink - Smart Home
Lifestyle

3 Use the app to set up the smart home hub and add and control your smart home devices

Registering with Apps

When a smart home device is installed and the related app downloaded to a smartphone or tablet, there is usually a requirement to register with the app's manufacturer before you can start using the app. There are two reasons for this:

- Registration identifies you as a customer of the device's manufacturer.

- Registration offers a wider range of functionality for the device, such as being able to contact it and control it remotely when you are away from home.

To register with a smart home device's app:

For a lot of smart devices you have to register before you can start using the device's app, or access it using a digital voice assistant.

1 Open the app and tap on the **Create Account** button

2 Enter the account details as required, usually including an email address and password that are entered in a single step or multiple steps in the account creation process. Tap on the **Submit** button to create a new account

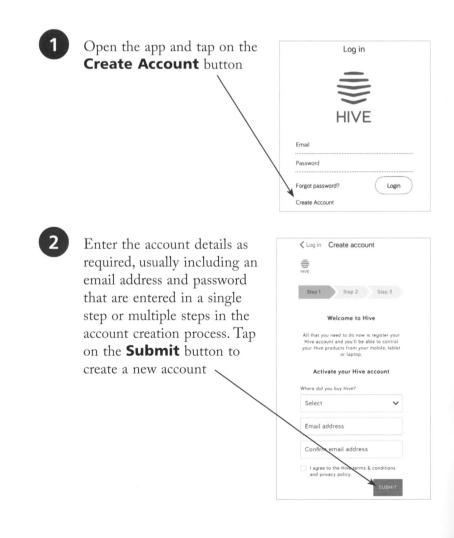

Using an online account

Once you have registered with a device's app it is possible to access your account details online. To do this:

1 Access the online website for your device and tap on the link to your own account

My Hue

2 Enter the sign-in details used to create the account and tap on the **Sign in** button

Some apps offer a range of functionality from their online sites. For others it is mainly a means of accessing a smart device remotely.

105

3 Details of your account are displayed

4 Tap on the options within the account page to view the various sections

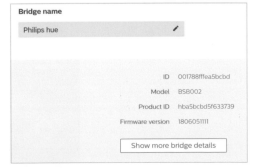

Using Multi-Device Apps

Some apps for smart home devices are designed to work with a range of smart home devices, rather than a single device that is created by the same manufacturer. To use multi-device apps:

Beware

Multi-device apps can be a good way to control a lot of devices from one place. However, they generally do not offer the same range of settings and functionality as a device's dedicated companion app.

1 Within the Apple App Store or Google Play Store, search for **smart home**

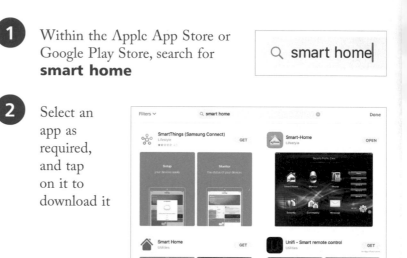

2 Select an app as required, and tap on it to download it

3 Multi-device apps can link to a range of smart home devices, including those controlling lighting, heating, security, music and communications

7 Smart Lighting

Smart lighting is one of the most accessible and effective ways to start using smart home devices. This chapter looks at using smart lighting and how it can be controlled in different ways.

About Smart Lighting

Smart lighting is one of the most accessible and affordable options for adding smart devices to the home: it can be set up in minutes, does not need an electrician (or any electrical knowledge), and creates a dramatic impact once it is up and running. Smart lighting also works impressively with digital voice assistants.

Elements of smart lighting

The good news about a smart lighting system is that all of the components can be linked to existing elements in your home, and there is no need to alter any current equipment. Smart lighting works through a controller (bridge) that is connected to your Wi-Fi router, and the smart light bulbs are then controlled by Wi-Fi through the bridge. The elements required for a smart lighting system include:

Smart light bulbs contain a considerable amount of technology and are more expensive than standard light bulbs. Single white bulbs are upwards of $10/£10.

- **Smart light bulbs**. These are light bulbs that can communicate using Wi-Fi via the smart lighting bridge. They can be either white, or white and colored, in which case they can change color and also create artistic scenes if more than one bulb is used in a particular room.

- **Bridge**. This is the controller that is connected to your Wi-Fi router. Once it has been set up, this is where commands will be sent (either through a related app or a digital voice assistant) and then distributed to the smart lighting system.

- **Remote control**. In addition to controlling the smart lighting through an app or a digital voice assistant, it can also be controlled with a remote control. This can be used to turn the lights on or off and dim them as required. If you have a group of smart lights in one room the remote control can usually only be used with the whole group, rather than control individual lights separately.

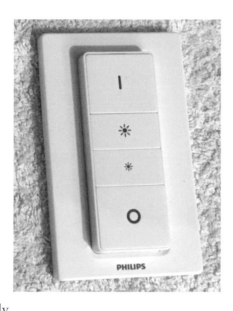

- **Smart lighting apps**. Most smart home devices have their own apps that can be used to control the devices. Smart lighting is no different, and all systems have their own companion apps. These can be used to control a range of functions: from turning lights on or off; to setting color scenes; and setting schedules for when lights are activated.

Hot tip

A good option for initially setting up a smart lighting system is to buy a starter pack. This will include a number of white or colored light bulbs, a bridge, and a remote control.

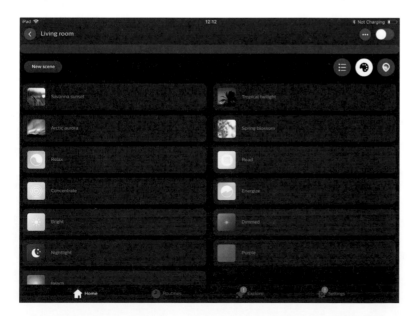

Getting Started

Smart lighting has a number of elements to it and there are a few steps that have to be done before it can be used. (The examples here are for the Philips Hue smart lighting system, which is one of the most popular options, but the process is similar for most major smart lighting systems.)

 Insert the smart light bulbs and turn the lights on at the wall light switch or a lamp switch (if applicable)

 Plug in the bridge and connect it to your Wi-Fi router using the supplied Ethernet cable

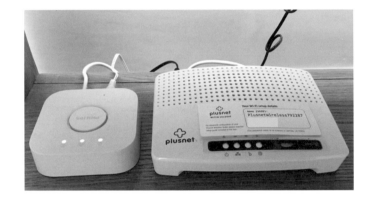

Some smart home devices can be controlled directly from their companion apps, without the need for a bridge. However, because smart lighting can involve several devices (light bulbs), they rely on the bridge to access the different elements.

 Download the related app, from either the Apple Store or the Google Play Store, to your smartphone or tablet

hue
PHILIPS

Philips Hue
Philips Lighting BV

GET

2.6 ★★★☆☆
268 Ratings

4 Open the app. It should locate the bridge automatically. Tap on the **Set up** button

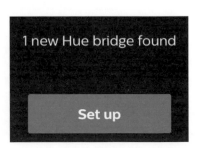

1 new Hue bridge found

Set up

5 Press the main button on the bridge to link it to the app

Close | Push-link

Press the push-link button on the Hue bridge you want to connect to.

6 The light bulbs that were inserted and turned on in Step 1 are listed in the **Light setup** section

Close | Light setup

Add light

Hue color lamp 1

Hue color lamp 2

Hue color lamp 3

Hue white lamp 1

Hue white lamp 2

Living room

Room has no lights

Hot tip

Scenes for smart lighting require two or more light bulbs in the same room in order to function properly. Also, it is best to have colored light bulbs to achieve the maximum effect of lighting scenes.

Setting up a Room

Once a smart lighting system has been set up and light bulbs have been added, rooms can be set up with the relevant light bulbs assigned to them. To do this:

 1 Open the smart lighting app

 2 Tap on the **Home** button on the bottom toolbar

 3 Tap on the **Create room** button

 4 Tap on the **Create new room** option

 5 The room is given a default name. To change this, tap on the **Room type** option

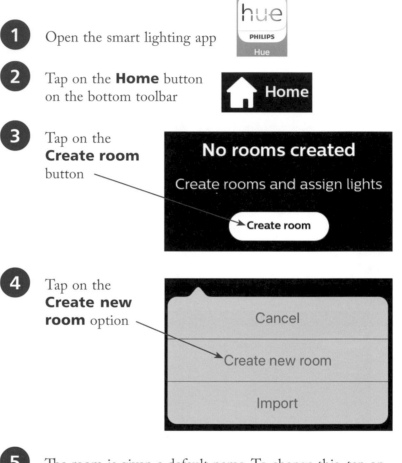

Don't forget

Once smart light bulbs have been installed and turned on, the light switch can be left on: all of the functionality of the bulb can be controlled through the light's app.

6 Tap on a room type and tap on the back button

7 Once the room type has been selected, light bulbs can be assigned to the room. Tap in the boxes to select the required light bulbs. Tap on the **Save** button to create the room, with the selected light bulbs

Beware

If you move the location of a smart light bulb, e.g. move it from the main light fitting in a room to a side lamp, the name and the functionality will not change. For instance, if the app thinks it is accessing Light 1, this will be unaffected regardless of which fitting the light is placed in, or even which room, if it has been moved to another room.

8 The new room is shown on the **Home** page

YOUR ROOMS

Living room
All lights are off

Using Lights

Individual light bulbs can be managed with the smart lighting app and they can also be controlled via a digital voice assistant, providing that the correct skills/actions have been added to the assistant. To get started using smart lights:

 Open the smart lighting app and tap on the **Home** button on the bottom toolbar

 Drag this button On to turn on all of the rooms, and their lights, that have been set up

 Tap on a room name to view details of the lights in the room

4 Tap on this button to view the individual lights in a room

5 Drag the buttons On or Off for individual lights, as required

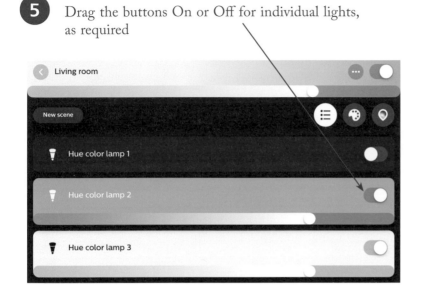

 The current color for a light bulb is shown in the window in Step 5.

6 Tap on this button to access available lighting scenes for the room

7 Tap on one of the scene options to apply that for all of the lights in room (for more details about Scenes, see pages 120-123)

Scenes can only be created with smart color light bulbs.

115

Customizing Lights

Because of the technology they contain, smart lights have great flexibility in terms of customizing the lights. This is particularly true for color smart light bulbs, as they can be set to almost any color that you want.

Dimming lights

Smart lights can be dimmed using a remote control by clicking on the dim button. This dims the lights incrementally each time that you click the button. Click on the button above the dim button to increase the brightness of a smart light.

Hot tip

Smart lights can be set to come on at a specific time and slowly get brighter, such as in the morning when you are waking up. This is done through the use of Routines. For more details about this, see pages 124-129.

In addition to using a remote control, smart lights can also be dimmed by using their app. To do this:

1 Open a room that has been set up on the smart light's app, as shown on page 112, and drag this button On

2 Drag the slider underneath the light's name to dim it (this has the same effect regardless of whether the light is a color one or a white one)

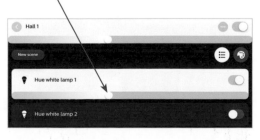

Customizing colors

The color of smart light bulbs can be customized to almost any one that you want. This can only be done with color smart light bulbs, not white ones. To do this:

1 Open a room that has been set up with color light bulbs, as shown on page 114. Tap on the room name. Tap on the name of a light bulb to access a color wheel

2 The current color used by the light bulb is indicated on the color wheel

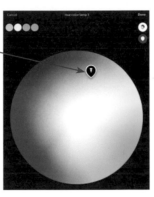

3 Drag the light's icon to a new position on the color wheel to use this color for the light bulb. Tap on the **Done** button

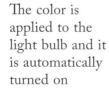

4 The color is applied to the light bulb and it is automatically turned on

Hot tip

When a new color is selected for a light bulb, previously selected colors are shown at the top left-hand side of the window. Tap on one of these to use it as the selected color again. This is a good option if you can't exactly remember what color was used before.

Hot tip

Light colors can also be changed with a digital voice assistant, using a command such as, "[Device wake word], turn hall to blue".

...cont'd

Changing light names

By default, smart light bulbs are usually given names based on their manufacturer and lamp number; e.g. Hue white lamp 1. However, this can becomes confusing if you have a large number of smart light bulbs and you want to edit or manage them. One option is to give then specific names so that they are associated with whichever room they are in. To do this:

Don't forget

Tap on the **Room setup** option in Step 2 to set up new rooms, using the **Create room** button, and add smart lights to them.

1 Open the smart lighting app and tap on the **Home** button on the bottom toolbar

2 Tap on the menu button on the top toolbar and select the **Light setup** option

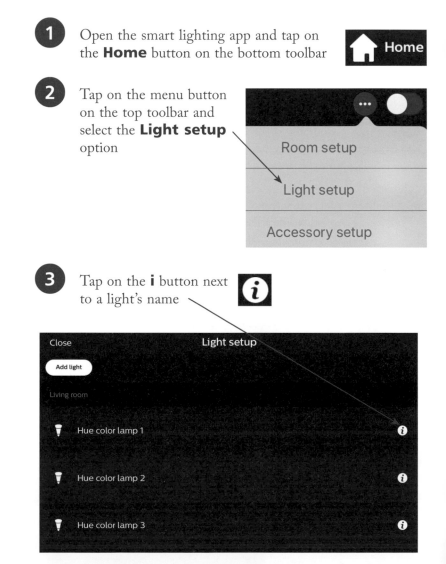

3 Tap on the **i** button next to a light's name

...cont'd

4 Details of
the light are
displayed,
including its
current name

5 Delete the default name and enter a new name, preferably
relating to the room in which the light is located

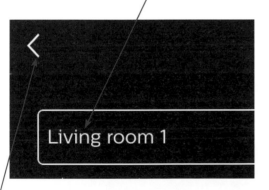

6 Tap on the back arrow

7 The light
bulb
is now
displayed
with its
new name.
Repeat
the
process to
rename
the other
lights

Tap on the **Add light**
button in Step 7 to add
a new smart light to an
existing room. The light
has to be powered on in
order for the app to be
able to discover it.

Smart Lighting Scenes

One of the great things about smart lights is that they can be set to a huge variety of colors, presuming that they are colored light bulbs. This can be done manually for individual light bulbs, and it is also possible to use preset scenes, with two or more colored bulbs. You can also create your own customized scenes. To use scenes:

Hot tip

Scenes are a great way to set a mood for a particular time of year, or for a specific type of movie or TV show.

1 Ensure that the colored light bulbs are installed, powered On and have been assigned to a room

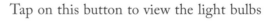

2 Open the smart lights' app and tap here to view a room containing the colored light bulbs

3 Tap on this button to view the light bulbs

4 Tap on this button to view the available scenes

5 The available preset scenes are displayed

6 Tap on a preset scene to apply it to the room

Don't forget

If you don't like a particular scene, simply tap on another one to change the overall lighting scheme.

7 Tap on the button in Step 3 to view the colors that have been applied to each light bulb in order to create the scene. Drag the sliders to edit the level of lighting for each light bulb, if required

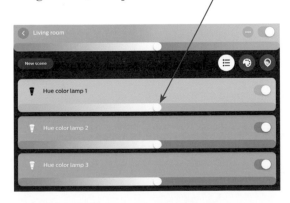

...cont'd

Creating custom scenes

In addition to using the preset color scenes, it is also possible to create your own customized ones. To do this:

 Access the room for which you want to create a new scene (as shown on page 120) and tap on the **New scene** button

 Tap here at the top of the window to create a name for the new scene

Cancel

Tap to enter scene name

Beware

You cannot use a scene name if it has already been used for one of the preset scenes.

122

 Enter a name for the new scene

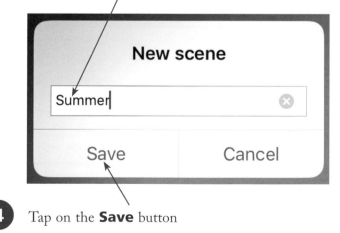

New scene

Summer

Save   Cancel

4 Tap on the **Save** button

5 Tap on this button at the bottom of the window to access the color wheel for selecting colors for individual light bulbs

6 Drag the light bulb icons on the color wheel to select colors for each bulb

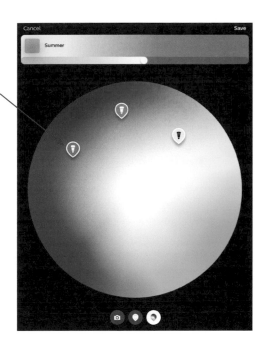

Hot tip

Tap on each light bulb icon in Step 6 to view its name at the top of the window. This is a good way to ensure that the correct colors are assigned to the intended light bulbs.

7 Tap on the **Save** button to create the new scene

Save

8 The new scene is added to the list of existing preset scenes and applied to the room automatically

Hot tip

Tap on this button at the bottom of the window in Step 6 to create a scene from a selection of photos, or one of your own photos on your smartphone or tablet.

Creating Routines

The flexibility of smart lighting does not end with the ability to change the color of smart light bulbs. It is also possible to create a range of routines, to turn lights on and off automatically, or set controls for when you are away from home. To use routines:

1 Open the smart lights' app and tap on the **Routines** button on the bottom toolbar

2 Tap on one of the routine categories to view the items within it

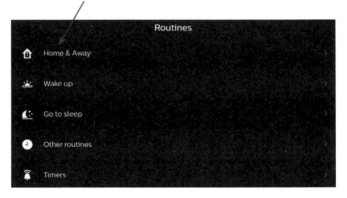

Waking up

Routines can be set to instruct smart lights to turn on slowly in the morning, at the time you would normally be waking up. This ensures that you get used to the light at a leisurely pace, rather than the bright light of a standard light bulb. To do this:

1 Access the **Routines** section as above and tap on the **Wake up** button

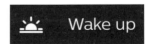

2 Tap on the **Create routine** button

For creating a wake up routine, the **Create routine** button only needs to be activated the first time that a routine is created. After an initial wake up routine has been created, there is a **Create wake up** button that can be used to set up another wake up routine.

3 Drag these barrels to set the time at which you want the smart lighting to first come on

4 Tap on the **Fade in** button to specify a time period for how long the smart lighting takes to get to full power

Color smart light bulbs are the best option for creating wake up routines, as they offer the optimum performance.

5 Tap on the **Where?** button to select the room in which you want the routine to be applied

6 Tap on a room to select it and tap on the back button

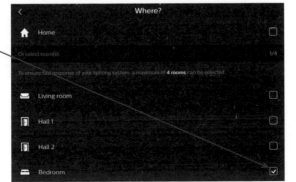

...cont'd

7 Tap on the room selected for the wake up routine, in the previous step

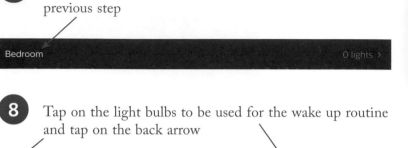

8 Tap on the light bulbs to be used for the wake up routine and tap on the back arrow

The **Go to sleep** routine can be used to set a time at which bedroom lights start to gradually dim, before you want to go to sleep. The process for creating this is the same as for creating a wake up routine.

9 Drag this button on to specify a time at which the lights turn off, after the wake up routine has been applied. Drag the barrels in the same way as setting a time in Step 3

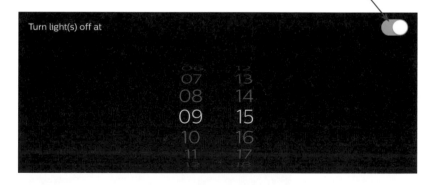

10 Tap on the **Save** button at the top of the window to create the new routine

Home & Away

If you have a habit of leaving household lights on when you leave home, or like to have the lights on ready for your return, the Home & Away feature is excellent. This enables you to set your lights to be turned off automatically when you leave home and turned on again just before you return. This is done using the location services feature on your smartphone or tablet: the smart lighting app communicates with your smartphone or tablet, and when it recognizes that you have left home, or are returning, the smart lighting app turns the lights on or off accordingly. To use the Home & Away feature:

Hot tip

The Home & Away feature requires you to be logged in to the online account of the smart lighting manufacturer. An account can be set up when you first start using the app, or from the **Log in** button when you first access Home & Away (on the login page there is also an option to create an account). Once you have registered for an account you can control your smart lighting remotely.

1 Ensure location services are turned On for the smart lighting app on your smartphone or tablet

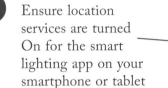

2 Open the smart lighting app, access the **Routines** section from the button on the bottom toolbar and tap on the **Home & Away** button

3 Drag the **Location aware** button On to enable the smart lighting app to access your location

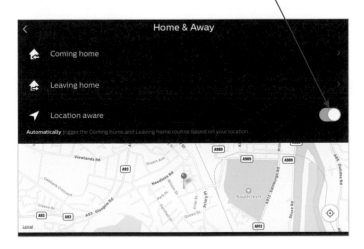

...cont'd

 Tap on the **Coming home** button

 Tap on the **Turn on** button to select rooms to which the function will be applied

Beware

All rooms can be selected to be turned on with the **Coming home** feature. However, it may not be necessary to do this every time that you return home, so it can be better to assign one or two rooms, rather than them all.

 Tap on the boxes next to the rooms to which you want to apply the Home & Away functionality

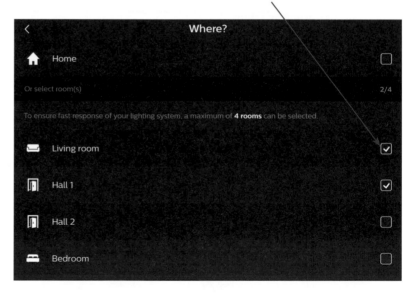

Don't forget

Other routines for turning smart lighting on or off automatically (and fading it in and out) can also be created based on a specific time of day or at sunset or sunrise, using the **Other routines** button in the Routines section.

 Tap on the back arrow

8 The rooms that have been added are listed on the Coming home page. The current lighting option is displayed at the right-hand side. Tap on one of the lights to change it

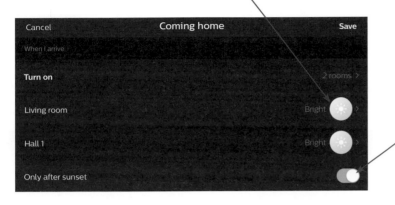

Beware

Drag the **Only after sunset** button On in Step 8 to ensure that the Coming home functionality is only applied after sunset, rather than at any time of day, during which the lights may not be needed to be turned on. Sunset is determined from the clock and location on your smartphone or tablet.

9 Tap on one of the default options for the settings for the lights when you come home. Alternatively, tap on one of the Scenes to apply this

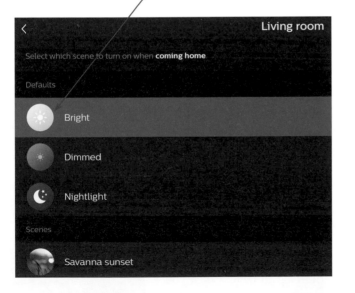

Hot tip

The process for creating a **Leaving home** routine only requires the affected rooms to be selected, since the lights will be turned off when you leave. For Leaving home it is worth selecting all rooms, so that no lights will be left on by mistake.

10 Tap on the back arrow in the top left-hand corner of the window, and tap on the **Save** button to use the selected Home & Away option

Settings

As with most computing devices and services, there is a range of settings that can be used with smart lighting. To use these:

1 Open the app and tap on the **Settings** button on the bottom toolbar

2 Tap on one of the **Settings** categories to view the items within it

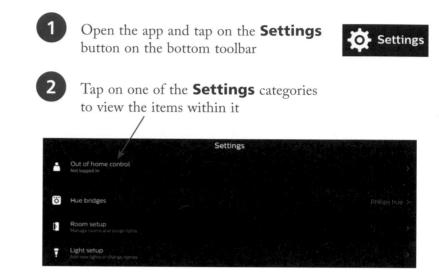

Some of the options to look at include:

Out of home control

Use this to log in to the online service for your smart lights, so that you can control them remotely.

1 Tap on the **Out of home control** button

2 Tap on the **Log in** button to log in to your online account with the smart lighting manufacturer, or create a new account from the Log in page. Once you have logged in you will be able to control your system remotely

A new account can be created with a smart lighting manufacturer when you first open the related app on your smartphone or tablet.

...cont'd

Hue bridges

This can be used to view details about the bridge that is being used for your smart lighting, and add new ones.

1 Tap on the **Hue bridges** button

2 Tap on the **i** icon to view details about your bridge, or tap on the **Add Hue bridge** button to add a new one

Hot tip

A new bridge can be set up for another person in a household, so that they have their own personal control over lights in a specific room.

131

Room setup

This can be used to assign lights to existing rooms, and also create new rooms to which lights can then be assigned.

1 Tap on the **Room setup** button

2 Tap on an existing room to view the lights that have been assigned to it, and add new lights, as required

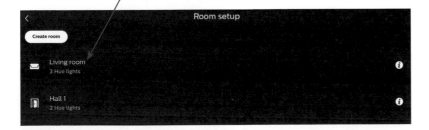

3 Tap on the **Create room** button to set up a new room and assign lights to it

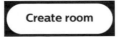

...cont'd

Light setup

This can be used to assign lights to existing rooms, and also create new rooms to which lights can then be assigned.

Tap on the **Light setup** button

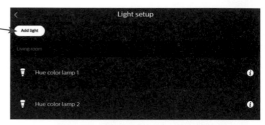

Tap on the **Add light** button to add a new light that has been installed

Once a new smart light bulb has been added to the app it can then be assigned to a room, using the room setup option as shown on page 131.

To add a new light, the smart light bulb has to be inserted in a socket and powered On. Tap on the **Search** button to enable the app to find the new smart light bulb, so that it is ready for use

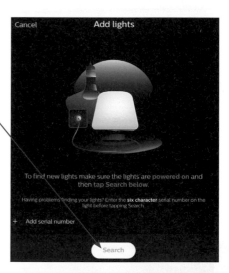

Tap on the **i** button in Step 2 to view details about a smart light bulb. Tap on the **Delete** button to remove it so that it cannot be discovered or assigned to a room

8 Smart Heating

Smart heating is an effective and cost-efficient way to control the heating in your home. This chapter looks at installing smart heating and shows how to apply settings and schedules so you have complete control over it.

About Smart Heating

Smart heating systems enable you to control your central heating with a wireless thermostat that can be managed through a related app, or with a digital voice assistant. Smart heating can also be controlled remotely, so that you always have the ability to monitor and manage your central heating.

Smart heating works with central heating systems, and the examples in this chapter use the widely used and popular Nest smart heating system.

A smart thermostat should be fitted by a qualified installer (several devices have their own recommended installers) and once it has been set up and connected to your home Wi-Fi, it can be used to control and manage your central heating in a number of different ways.

- Turn your heating on or off (either through an app or by using a digital voice assistant, using a command such as "[Device name], turn heating on/off").

- Set your smart thermostat to a specific temperature setting.

- Program your smart thermostat to come on or go off at specific times. This can be as many times as you like during the day.

- Turn your heating on or off remotely (using the app).

- Use an economy setting so that you can keep your heating on without wasting unnecessary energy.

- Apply a frost setting when you are away from home, if you are worried about freezing pipes.

Some smart thermostats can also learn from heating settings that you have used before. For instance, if you regularly have the temperature at the same level when you return home at a certain time, the smart thermostat will learn to set this automatically. They can also have settings applied to determine whether you are home or not and set the temperature accordingly. This helps to save energy, which is one of the benefits of a smart thermostat.

Elements of Smart Heating

Smart heating enables you to control the heating in your home through an app or a digital voice assistant. This can be done while you are at home, and also remotely. The elements of a smart heating system include:

- A heat link thermostat that connects to the central heating boiler. The heating system is then left on at the boiler: all of the control is done through the heat link thermostat, using an app, a system controller (learning thermostat), or a digital voice assistant.

Beware

The heat link and smart thermostat should be fitted by an approved central heating engineer or gas fitter.

135

- A learning thermostat (smart thermostat) that communicates with the heat link connected to the central heating system. The learning thermostat is able to monitor room temperatures and adjust them accordingly.

Smart Heating App

A companion app is required to set up and manage a smart heating system (in this case the Nest app, which can be downloaded to a smartphone or a tablet from the Apple App Store or the Google Play Store). To use the app:

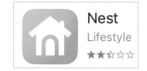

Nest
Lifestyle
★★✩✩✩

Don't forget

Similar options to those accessible through the app can also be used on the learning thermostat for controlling heating.

Don't forget

Before the heating controls on these two pages can be used, the smart thermostat has to first be linked to the app. See pages 138-141 for details about this.

1 Open the app and tap on the **Heating** button to access the basic heating controls

Home
Home

Heating
OFF

2 Tap on the **Heat** button or **Off** button as required

To adjust the temperature, choose a different thermostat mode.

 Heat

 Off   ✓

Cancel

3 Tap on the **Schedule** button on the bottom toolbar to create a schedule for when the heating comes on or goes off, automatically

The bottom toolbar contains buttons for Mode, Eco, Schedule and History (see also image in Step 1 on page 154).

4 Tap on the **History** button on the bottom toolbar to view a chart of your energy usage

The items on these two pages are looked at in more details throughout this chapter.

137

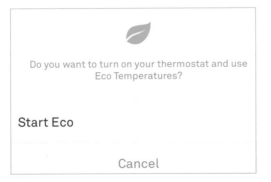

5 Tap on the **Eco** button on the bottom toolbar to access economy mode for saving energy

Adding a Smart Thermostat

Before a smart heating system can be used with an app it has to have the smart thermostat added to it. To do this:

The smart thermostat has to be installed and powered On before it can be added to the companion app.

1 Open the smart heating app on your smartphone or tablet and tap on the **Add product** button

2 The smartphone or tablet's camera can be used to scan the product code of the learning thermostat. Tap on the **OK** button to give the app permission to use the camera

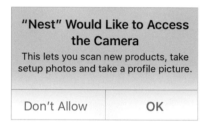

"Nest" Would Like to Access the Camera

This lets you scan new products, take setup photos and take a profile picture.

Don't Allow	OK

3 Position the camera so that the code on the learning thermostat is visible for the camera. The camera will capture the code automatically when it is clearly visible

Position the code within the green square when the camera is capturing the code.

4 Tap on the **Start installation** button

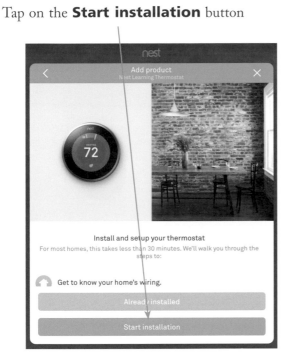

5 Tap on the applicable product

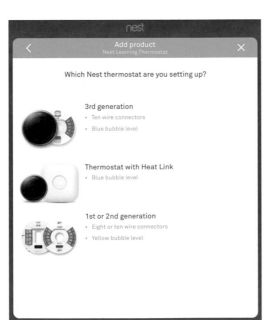

Hot tip

Several products can be added for the same manufacturer. However, they each have to be added separately, using the same process as for adding a smart thermostat shown on these pages.

...cont'd

 6 When the smart thermostat is installed and connected to your heating system, tap on the **Next** button

The product key can be obtained from the learning thermostat's Settings section.

 7 Enter the required product key

When a correct product key is entered, the setup process will move on to the next screen automatically.

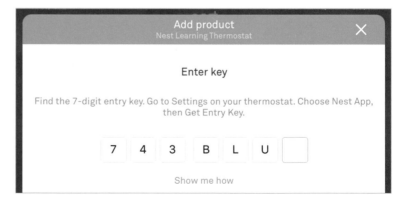

8 Tap on the **Done** button to complete the installation

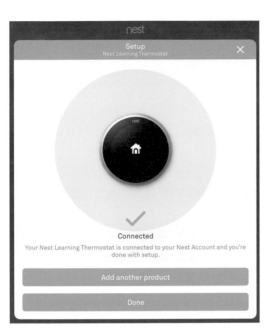

9 The smart thermostat is displayed on the Homepage of the smart heating app

Don't forget

The Home button in Step 9 refers to settings for when you are at home. There are also options for applying settings for when you are away from home. See pages 154-156 for details.

Setting the Temperature

Once the smart thermostat has been set up and added to the smart heating app, the app can then be used to control and manage the heating system. One of the most obvious options is for turning the heating on and off and setting the temperature. To do this:

 Open the smart heating app and tap on the **Heating** button on the Homepage

 The heating controls are displayed in the right-hand panel of the app

If the smart thermostat is not connected to your home Wi-Fi network, the **Home** button will display as **Offline**.

 Tap in the center of the main control dial

4 Tap on the **Heat** button to turn the heating on

To adjust the temperature, choose a different thermostat mode.

≋ Heat

≋ Off ✓

Cancel

5 The current temperature set for the smart thermostat is shown in the center of the control dial. If the temperature is less than the recorded outside temperature, the heating will not be activated

The readout on the app is the same as on the learning thermostat. The temperature can also be changed on the learning thermostat by rotating the outer ring on the body of the device.

6 Drag on this marker to change the temperature of the heating system. When the temperature is above the outside temperature, the heating will turn on, indicated by the display turning orange

The temperature can also be changed by tapping on the up and down arrows at the bottom of the control dial.

Creating a Schedule

A smart heating system can have a timed schedule created for it so that changes are applied automatically during the day. Settings can be applied for the temperature of the system and also the times at which the temperature is activated. To do this:

 Open the smart heating app and tap on the **Schedule** button on the bottom toolbar of Heating page, as shown on page 137

 The default schedule is shown

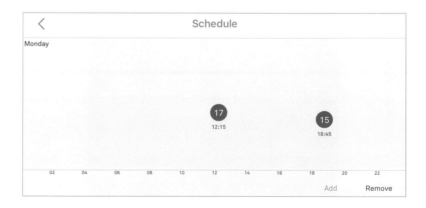

 Tap on an individual day to select settings for the schedule for that day

---

Beware

A schedule will only be activated when the smart heating is on.

...cont'd

4 Press and hold on the temperature icon for the specific day and drag the icon up or down to change the temperature settings

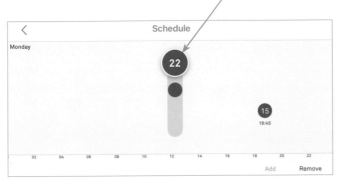

There will be a maximum and a minimum temperature that can be set, depending on your heating system.

5 Drag the icon left or right to change the time at which the temperature will be applied

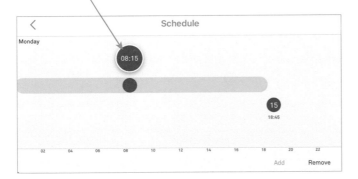

6 Changes to the current schedule are displayed

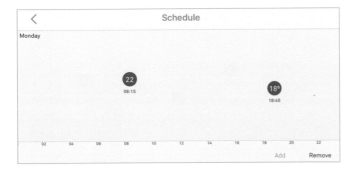

...cont'd

7 Tap on the **Add** button at the bottom of the Schedule window to add more timings and temperatures

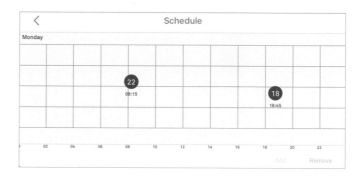

8 A grid is displayed on the Schedule page

The **Add** button in Step 7 has to be selected each time a new scheduling point is added.

9 Tap on a point on the grid to add a new heating icon

...cont'd

10 Add as many new scheduling points as required and apply a time and temperature for each of them

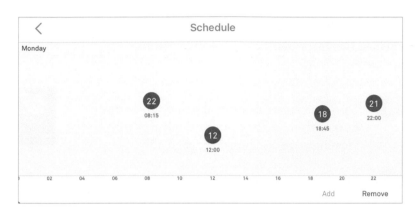

11 Once all of the relevant items have been added, tap on the back arrow in the top left-hand corner of the Schedule page

12 The new schedule is displayed. Tap on each day to add the specific schedule details

Day						
Monday		22	12		18	21
Tuesday			17		15	
Wednesday			17		15	
Thursday			17		15	
Friday			17		15	
Saturday						
Sunday						

Copy Week

13 Tap on the **Copy Week** button to copy the current schedule and paste it into another week

Applying Eco Settings

Saving energy is an important feature of any heating system, and a smart heating system can achieve this with the Eco setting. This is designed to recognize when there is no one at home, and adjust the temperature accordingly. It will maintain a lower temperature so that your home is still heated, while using less energy than the scheduled temperature. To use the Eco setting:

Don't forget

Eco mode is indicated by a green leaf on the main control dial.

Hot tip

The current Eco temperature is indicated by this bar on the main control dial.

1 Open the smart heating app and tap on the **Eco** button on the bottom toolbar of the Heating page, as shown on page 137

2 Tap on the **Start Eco** button

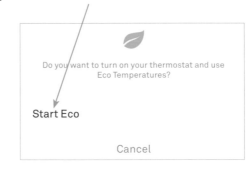

Do you want to turn on your thermostat and use Eco Temperatures?

Start Eco

Cancel

3 The Eco setting is displayed on the main control dial

23

ECO

...cont'd

Setting the Eco temperature

The temperature for the Eco mode can be set when the smart heating system is first set up. It can also be changed within the Settings section. To do this:

 1 Open the smart heating app and tap on the **Settings** button on the Heating Homepage

2 Tap on the **Eco Temperatures** option in the Heating settings

Eco Temperatures

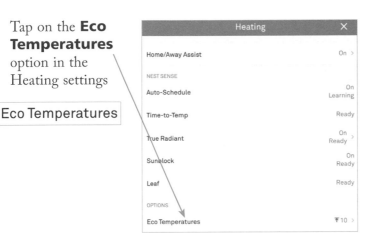

3 Drag this slider to change the Eco temperature

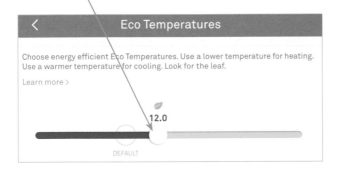

4 On the Heating Homepage, tap on the **Eco** button in Step 1 on the previous page, and tap on the **Stop Eco** option to turn off Eco mode

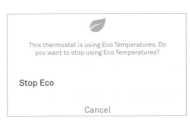

Don't forget

If the heating system is on, the Eco setting will be applied automatically if the smart thermostat identifies that there is no one at home. If it is turned on manually, as shown on the previous page, the Eco setting will be applied (providing it is above the current outside temperature). If the heating system is off, the Eco setting will not be applied (unless it is for the Safety setting, see page 153).

Hot tip

Activating Eco mode automatically when there is no one at home can be specified in the Settings section of the smart heating app. See page 150 for details.

149

Smart Heating Settings

A number of elements of a smart heating system can be customized, so that you have complete control over the system and can set it up the way that you want. To do this:

Don't forget

The **Settings** button is located in the top right-hand corner of the smart heating app's Homepage (see image in Step 1 on page 142).

Don't forget

The **Time-to-Temp** setting is used to display the time that the system will take to reach the required temperature.

Time-to-Temp

1 Open the smart heating app and tap on the **Settings** button on the Heating Homepage

2 Tap on the **Home/Away Assist** option to enable Eco mode when there is no one in your home

Home/Away Assist

3 Drag the **Automatically use Eco temperatures when no one's home?** button to On to enable Eco mode to be activated automatically when there is no one in your home

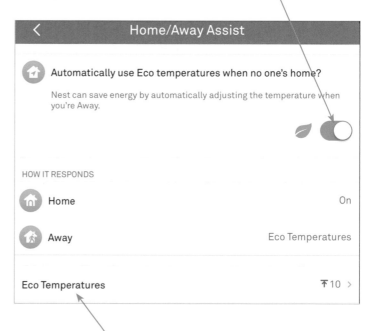

4 Tap on the **Eco Temperatures** button to specify the temperature for Eco mode when no one is home

5 Tap on the **Auto-Schedule** option and drag the button to On, to enable your system to automatically create a heating schedule based on how you use your heating

Auto-Schedule

Auto-Schedule

Auto-Schedule learns your behavior as you adjust your thermostat and automatically creates a schedule to match your heating preferences.

6 Tap on the **True Radiant** option and drag the **True Radiant** button to On, to enable your system to learn how long it takes to reach the specified temperature and react accordingly

True Radiant

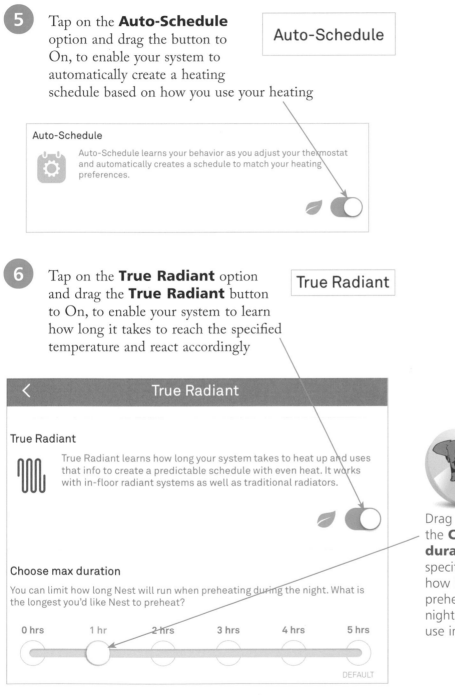

<   True Radiant

True Radiant

True Radiant learns how long your system takes to heat up and uses that info to create a predictable schedule with even heat. It works with in-floor radiant systems as well as traditional radiators.

Choose max duration

You can limit how long Nest will run when preheating during the night. What is the longest you'd like Nest to preheat?

| 0 hrs | 1 hr | 2 hrs | 3 hrs | 4 hrs | 5 hrs |

DEFAULT

Don't forget

Drag the button under the **Choose max duration** heading to specify a time period for how long the system preheats during the night, in preparation for use in the morning.

...cont'd

Certain adjustments can also be made using the learning smart thermostat and may not be available via the app.

The **Leaf** option should be set up automatically. However, if it is not displayed, it will be possible to activate it in the Leaf setting.

 7 Tap on the **Sunblock** button to specify an action if the learning smart thermostat is positioned in the sun

Sunblock

8 Drag the **Sunblock** button to On, to enable the learning smart thermostat to recognize when it is in the sun and adjust the heating accordingly

Sunblock

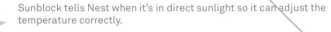

Sunblock tells Nest when it's in direct sunlight so it can adjust the temperature correctly.

9 Tap on the **Leaf** button to view the details of what this signifies when it is displayed

Leaf

Leaf

Leaf appears when you have adjusted Nest to an energy-saving temperature.

10 Tap on the **Temperature units** button and tap on the **F** or **C** buttons to display the default temperature in Fahrenheit or Celsius

Temperature units

Temperature units

°F | °C

11 Tap on the **Equipment** button to view details about the **Heat source** of the heating system and the **Heat type**

Equipment

Equipment	
Heat source	Gas
Heat type	Radiator
Safety Temperature	⤒4

12 Tap on the **Safety Temperature** button

Equipment	
Heat source	Gas
Heat type	Radiator

Safety Temperature

Nest will activate heat at the safety minimum, even when the thermostat is set to OFF.

This can keep your plumbing from freezing.

4.0

DEFAULT

Don't forget

If the thermostat measures a temperature below the safety temperature in Step 13, the heating will be activated at the level that has been specified.

13 Drag this slider to specify a minimum safety temperature. This will be activated even if the smart thermostat is off, and is designed to prevent pipes from freezing

Home and Away

In order for the Home and Away functionality of a smart heating system to work properly, the system has to have a way of knowing when you are away from home. This can be done manually (see tip) and it can also be linked to the location of your smartphone: if it recognizes that your phone is in a different location it will activate the Away mode for the smart heating system. To set this up on your smartphone:

Hot tip

To manually tell the smart heating system that you are away from home, tap on the **Home** button on the app's Homepage and then tap on the **Away** button.

1 Tap on the **Heating** button to return to the Homepage of the app

2 Tap on the **Settings** button in the top right-hand corner of the Homepage

3 Tap on the **Home/Away Assist** option

Home	✕
👤 Account	>
🏠 Home info	>
🏠 Home/Away Assist	>

4 The Home/Away Assist option has tabs for Home and Away. These can be used to specify options for the heating for these two options. Tap on the **Heating** button to select the required heating mode

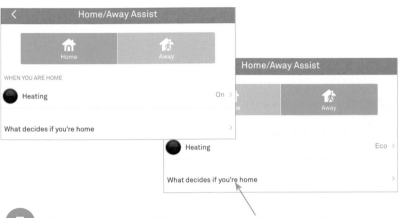

Make sure that the Heating setting for Away is set to Eco, otherwise there will be no benefit from the Away settings as it will be the same as the Home one.

5 Under either the Home or Away tab, tap on the **What decides if you're home** option

6 Tap on the **Use phone location** option

> **What decides**
>
> The products in your home can use phone location and product sensors to figure out if you're Home or Away.
>
> Learn more >
>
> THIS HOME
>
> Use phone location   No
>
> PRODUCTS
>
> ● Heating   Yes

7 Tap on the **OK** button to continue with the Home/Away Assist wizard for adding your phone's location

...cont'd

 8 Tap on the **Use phone** button to use your phone's location to determine whether you are at home or away

> **This feature needs permission to use your location.**
>
> When you enable this, Nest will use your phone's location to help determine if you're home or away. This will be used for any of your homes that use Home/Away Assist.
>
> Learn more
>
> Don't use   Use phone

The **Always Allow** option needs to be selected in Step 9, so that your smartphone's location can be used even if the smart heating app is not running.

156

 9 Tap on the **Always Allow** button to enable the smart heating app to access your phone's location, even when the app is not running

> **Allow "Nest" to access your location?**
> This helps your products know when you come and go, even when the Nest app isn't running.
>
> Only While Using the App
>
> Always Allow
>
> Don't Allow

Location Services have to be turned on for the smart heating app within the smartphone's Settings, so that the smart heating app can communicate with the smartphone and use its location.

10 The **Use phone location** button is On, indicating that the smartphone's location can be tracked by the app and the smart heating system amended as required

> <   What decides
>
> The products in your home can use phone location and product sensors to figure out if you're Home or Away.
> Learn more >
>
> THIS HOME
>
> Use phone location
> When enabled, the Nest products at this home (Home) will use participating phones to help figure out if anyone is home.
> Learn more >
>
> PEOPLE
>
> 👤 You   Yes >
> Nick's iPhone 8
>
> PRODUCTS
>
> ⚫ Heating   Yes

9 Smart Security

This chapter looks at how to use smart security devices around the home to make it as secure as possible.

Smart Security Cameras

Security is a major issue for any home owner, and it is important to know that your home is as secure as possible. In addition to burglar alarms and security lights, it is also possible to install security cameras that you can monitor on your smartphone or tablet and keep an eye on your home even when you are away.

There are various smart security cameras on the market, varying in functionality and cost. However, in order to create a smart security camera system that will provide a good degree of protection, some of the following elements should be included:

High-quality cameras

Cameras can be affixed around the exterior of your home, and property, so that they can video anything that is taking place. These are usually fixed in one spot and offer a single view. It is worth getting as high a quality as possible as this will ensure a better picture quality and images will be clearer. Also, it is important to use cameras that can capture

images in the dark using infrared, or a night vision equivalent.

If the camera does not have night vision then it will be inactive for approximately half of the day. Ideally, look for a system with a minimum of two cameras; one for the front of your property and one for the back. Some security cameras are designed specifically for outdoor or indoor use, while others are designed for both.

158

Communication functionality

Some smart security cameras can also double up as smart doorbells: when there is someone at your door, you can have a two-way video conversation with them through the camera, if it has a communication function.

Face recognition

One of the functions of smart security cameras is to send an alert to your phone when it recognizes someone approaching your property. In order to ensure that this does not happen for people that you know such as family members, look for a system that uses face recognition so that you can set it up to ignore certain people and only alert you when strangers are near your property.

A hard drive for storing footage

No one wants to constantly look at video of their home. This means that some instances of dubious behavior around the property could be missed (unless the camera has an alert function for identifying unwanted people). One option is to use a system which links to a hard drive, so that the video footage is stored here and can be reviewed once it has been captured. Look for a hard drive that can store a minimum of 24 hours of footage.

Cloud storage

Some smart camera manufacturers also offer a cloud backup service. This is a subscription service (usually monthly or yearly) that offers storage and backup for your camera footage. So, if there is anything amiss, it can be reviewed from the cloud storage.

Companion app

Smart security cameras need a companion app, which can be used to view footage from the camera and also receive alerts and notifications from the camera. The companion apps can be downloaded from the Apple App Store or the Google Play Store to your smartphone or tablet. The app can also be used to apply a range of settings for the camera.

Don't forget

Smart security cameras need to be connected to the home Wi-Fi network in order to be able to communicate with its companion app on a smartphone or tablet.

Hot tip

Some manufacturers produce a range of smart home devices; e.g. smart lighting, smart heating and smart security cameras. If this is the case, a single companion app should be able to be used to control all of the different devices.

Smart Alarm Systems

Some manufacturers provide full smart alarm systems that can be controlled through an app on your smartphone or tablet. Some of the elements of these include:

- **Wall-mounted alarm**. This is what goes off if unexpected activity is detected by the alarm sensors. The alarm will flash and emit a sound when it is activated.

Smart alarm systems usually connect to your home Wi-Fi network using a smart hub that communicates with the smart alarm components.

160

- **Smart alarm app**. This is the companion app for the smart alarm system. Once it has been downloaded to your smartphone or tablet it can be used to arm and disarm the alarm system. The app can also be used to configure the alarm to your own requirements.

- **Manual control unit**. This is located within the home, and used to manually arm and disarm the alarm and apply settings.

- **Internal door and window sensors**. These are used to determine if doors and windows have been opened while the alarm is armed. If this happens, the wall-mounted alarm will be activated and an appropriate alert will be sent to the app on your smartphone or tablet.

Beware

Always check that a smart alarm system is disarmed before you go into your home, in case you set if off inadvertently. Checking the status of the alarm can be done using the device's companion app.

- **Internal motion sensors**. These are used to detect movement in the home while the alarm is armed. If this happens, the wall-mounted alarm will be activated and an appropriate alert will be sent to the app on your smartphone or tablet.

Indoor Security

Indoor smart cameras can be used to monitor individual rooms in the home. This could be used for reassurance in terms of babies, infants or elderly relations who are in different rooms of the home. Some features to look for in indoor security cameras are:

- **High-quality video images**. The higher the quality the better, as it will provide a clearer and sharper image.

- **Night vision**. For indoor smart cameras it is important to have night vision, as much of the time that you will want to access the camera will be at night; e.g. when a baby is sleeping.

- **Camera rotation**. Look for smart cameras that can be rotated automatically, so that you can view the whole room. The rotation of the camera can be controlled using the companion app on your smartphone or tablet.

- **Motion detection**. Some smart cameras have a motion sensor that can detect movement in a room. If this happens, an alert is sent to the camera's app on your smartphone or tablet.

- **Two-way communication**. Some smart cameras can also be used as video communication devices, if they have the functionality so that someone can speak through the camera and someone else can reply through it.

Beware

If you install a smart camera into a child's room, or an adult's, tell them that the camera is there and why you have installed it.

Video Doorbell

Video doorbells not only give you peace of mind in terms of viewing who is at your door; they also enable you to talk to people when they are waiting to come in. The elements of a video doorbell are:

- **The physical doorbell**. This is affixed at a convenient position at the front or back door. This contains a standard doorbell and also a video camera that records visitors once they have pressed the bell.

Position the video doorbell so that the camera can clearly see anyone who is in front of the door.

- **The video doorbell's companion app**. This is used to view the video feed from the doorbell. It can also be used to speak to the people who are waiting at the door. They should be able to communicate with you too, using the internal microphone in the video doorbell.

Some video doorbells also have motion sensors, so that they can identify callers and activate the video camera, even if people do not press the bell.

Smart Locks

Smart locks do away with the need to use a physical key to get into your home. They can be operated in a number of ways:

- **Using an app on your smartphone or tablet**. This can be used to lock or unlock the door from either inside the home or remotely.

- **Using a digital voice assistant**. Devices such as Amazon Alexa can have skills added to them so that locks can be locked or unlocked with a voice command, such as, "Alexa, lock/unlock the back door".

- **Using a biometric fingerprint keypad**. Individual fingerprints can be recorded by the smart lock so that only these can be used to open the lock.

- **Using a smart card**. A smart card can be used to lock or unlock a door by swiping over the sensor on the lock.

- **Using a smart fob**. A smart fob, such as one used on a key ring, can be used in a similar way to a smart card.

- **Using a numeric keypad on the lock**. A unique code can be created to be used with the smart lock.

Always ensure that there is at least one manual method of getting into your home, without having to rely exclusively on smart devices.

Check the specifications of a smart lock to ensure that it can be fitted to your doors.

10 More Smart Home Options

This chapter shows how to use robotic lawnmowers and vacuum cleaners, and some miscellaneous smart devices.

About Smart Plugs

Smart plugs are a small but effective way of controlling electrical devices around the home. They are easy to set up, which can usually be done without the need of a separate hub or bridge connected to your Wi-Fi router. However, there still needs to be a wireless option for the plug's companion app so that it can communicate with the app. Some options for smart plugs include:

- Turning devices on or off.

- Creating timed schedules to turn devices on or off automatically.

- Checking the status of electronic devices, via the smart plug.

- Using remote access with a companion app.

Once smart plugs have been installed they can be linked to digital voice assistants so that they can be activated using voice controls. They can also be controlled using an app on a smartphone or a tablet.

Hot tip

Smart plugs are an excellent option for ensuring that all of your electrical devices are turned off when you are away from home. If in doubt, check on the app and turn off any smart plugs that are on.

Smart plugs have to be installed and powered on in order for apps and digital voice assistants to be able to communicate with them. Once they have been set up, there is a green light on the smart plug that indicates that the plug is powered on and connected to the required wireless network.

Using a smart plug

The functionality of a smart plug can be accessed from a linked digital voice assistant and the plug's companion app:

1 Open the app to view the status of the plug and turn it On or Off

2 Tap on the plug to view its details, such how long it has been in operation

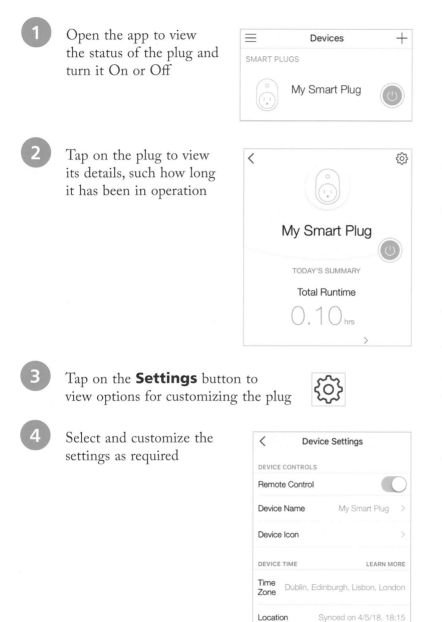

3 Tap on the **Settings** button to view options for customizing the plug

4 Select and customize the settings as required

Hot tip

It is important for smart plugs to have a remote control function, and for the plug to be turned on, so that it can be accessed remotely. If remote control is turned off, the plug will only be available on your home network, not remotely; i.e. if you are accessing it from your smartphone over a 3G/4G network.

Robotic Lawnmowers

One of the main reasons for installing smart home devices is to make life easier for ourselves. This can be by automating a number of tasks, and also using smart home devices to perform chores that we do not like. For many people, this includes cutting the grass. To solve this problem, robotic lawnmowers can be used to cut the grass automatically. The elements of a robotic lawnmower include:

Don't forget

If a robotic lawnmower meets an obstacle, such as a tree, it will bump off it, turn around and proceed in another direction.

168

- **The robotic lawnmower**. This is the device that cuts the grass. It is battery charged, which can be recharged at the charging station – see below.

- **Charging station**. This is the base station that is connected to a power source and is used to charge the robotic lawnmower. When the mower is in operation it will return to the charging station automatically to recharge.

- **Boundary wire**. This is a wire that is laid out around the perimeter of the garden. When the lawnmower reaches the boundary wire, it reverses and sets off in another direction.

Hot tip

When the robotic lawnmower is used for the first time, keep an eye on its operation to ensure that the boundary wire is positioned correctly. Reposition the wire if required.

- **Guide wire**. This is similar to the boundary wire and is used to guide the robotic lawnmower back to the charging station when it needs to be recharged.

- **Control panel**. This is the panel on the robotic lawnmower that can be used to apply settings for the device.

Setting up a robotic lawnmower

A robotic lawnmower requires a certain amount of initial setup. However, once this has been done, the device can be left to cut the grass without any further intervention. To set up a robotic lawnmower, ready for use:

1 Lay out the boundary wire around the perimeter of the lawn. Use the plastic pegs to attach the wire

2 Use a hammer to bang the pegs into the grass, so that they are as flush as possible to the ground

Beware

If the boundary wire is on the grass next to a flat surface, such as a path, it can be reasonably close to the edge of the grass (approximately 10cm) since the lawnmower will be able to move over the edge without cutting the flat surface. However, if there is a drop at the edge of the grass the boundary wire should be a greater distance from the edge (approximately 50cm) to prevent the lawnmower falling over the edge.

...cont'd

 Place the charging station in a position where it will be easy for the robotic lawnmower to reach it, for recharging

Once the charging station has been positioned, it can be attached to the ground with three large pegs.

 Run the guide wire directly away from the front of the charging station

The guide wire is threaded underneath the charging station and then connected at the back, see next page.

5 Cut the guide wire at a point where it can be joined to the boundary wire

6 Use one of the wire connectors to join the boundary wire and the guide wire

Beware

Ensure that the blue section of the connector in Step 5 is pressed fully down over the wires that have been inserted, to make sure that the connector joins the wires firmly enough.

7 Attach the wire connectors to the ends of two sections of the boundary wire and the guide wire

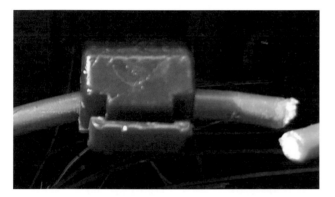

Don't forget

The guide wire connects in the middle of the two sections of the boundary wire: one section runs from the left-hand side of the charging station and is cut at the point when it meets the guide wire. Another section of boundary wire then runs to the right-hand side of the charging station. In the wire connector in Step 5, the boundary wire is positioned in the left-hand and right-hand connectors, and the guide wire is positioned in the middle connector.

8 Connect the wire connectors to the back of the charging station, following the instructions that have been provided, to ensure they are connected correctly. This creates what is known as the boundary loop

...cont'd

Don't forget

The robotic lawnmower uses three small, sharp, blades to cut the grass. These are located on a disc underneath the lawnmower. The blades cut off small pieces of grass and these mulch back into the lawn, and so no grass cuttings need to be collected.

9 If the boundary loop has been created successfully, a green light will appear on the charging station when it is connected to a power source

10 Place the robotic lawnmower on the charging station to charge it initially, before it starts cutting

11 Press the **Stop** button on the top of the robotic lawnmower to access the control panel

12 The control panel can be used to apply settings and instruct the robotic lawnmower to start operation

A PIN code can be used to lock the robotic lawnmower, in case it is stolen, in which case it could not be used without the PIN code.

13 Turn the button above the control panel to adjust the blade length for cutting the grass

Set the blade length to its highest level initially, to ensure that it does not cut the boundary wire or the guide wire. Once both of these have been grown over by the grass, start to lower the blade cutting length.

14 Press the **Start** button in Step 12 to instruct the robotic lawnmower to begin cutting the lawn. It will start its operation once it is sufficiently charged

A robotic lawnmower can be operated remotely if the power source is connected to a smart plug. Turn the plug on using its companion app to activate the robotic lawnmower.

Robotic Vacuum Cleaners

Doing the vacuuming around the home is not a task that many people look at fondly. However, like with cutting the grass, this chore can now be passed on to a robotic helper. Robotic vacuum cleaners are now widely available and, although they are generally still more expensive than their manual counterparts, they provide a genuine alternative to doing it yourself. As with most devices, robotic vacuum cleaners vary in terms of functionality and performance depending on how much you want to spend on one, but some of the features to consider are:

- **Navigation**. The best robotic vacuum cleaners navigate their way around your home, and any objects within it, using a combination of cameras and sensors. Look for a camera that has 360-degree vision, as this helps it map out the room and plan its course.

- **Cleaning**. Robotic vacuum cleaners should have brushes that extend along the width of the device, so that they can clean edges as they move along them. Also, some devices are thin enough so that they can go underneath furniture.

Check the suction specifications of a robotic vacuum cleaner to ensure that it is as strong as possible. The stronger the suction, the more likely it is that it will to be able to pick up stubborn items from carpets.

- **Mobility**. Wheels are good for robotic vacuum cleaners to get around the home, but even better are tank-type tracks that can be used to move over uneven surfaces and bumps.

- **Charging**. Robotic vacuum cleaners run on batteries, so a charging station is also an important accessory. Ideally, the device should be able to recognize when the battery is running low, and return to its charging station automatically.

Don't forget

Some robotic vacuum cleaners have companion apps that can be used to set a schedule and control the device remotely. The apps can also display reports of the work that the robotic vacuum cleaner has performed.

Miscellaneous Smart Devices

For most devices in the home there is a smart version that can be controlled through an app or a digital voice assistant. If there is not one on the market, there probably will be reasonably soon. Some smart devices that are already available include:

- **Smart kettles**. Boil your kettle hands-free using an app or a voice command.

Smart kettles can be ideal for new parents, as they can boil a kettle of water, hands-free, while holding their baby.

- **Smart air conditioning**. Keep your home, and yourself, cool with a smart air-conditioning unit. Some of them are static, while others can be moved around the home.

- **Smart smoke/carbon monoxide detectors**. Unlike traditional smoke/carbon monoxide detectors, the smart versions can alert you to an issue when you are away from home.

- **Smart garage opening**. Use an app to open garage doors that are fitted with a smart opening device. It is also possible to set the app so that it will recognize when the car is approaching the garage (using location services) and open the doors.

If you control your smart garage opening device from an app while you are in your car, make sure that you are not driving at the time.

- **Smart fridges**. Use a smart fridge to control and monitor its functionality. Some can also monitor what is being kept inside it and reorder items from their barcodes.

Smart Entertainment

Smart entertainment is provided through smart televisions that have the capability to connect to the internet. Once this has been done, it is then possible to subscribe to a wide range of online entertainment services and have all of your favorite online content broadcast through your TV.

Streaming services such as Netflix can be viewed through a smart TV. However, there is a subscription fee for a lot of these types of services.

Smart TVs

An increasing number of TVs are internet-enabled; i.e. smart TVs. Once they have been connected, you can start to sample the range of content that they offer.

There are two options for connecting a smart TV to the internet:

The newer the TV, the more chance there is that it will have a built-in Wi-Fi adapter, so that you can connect to the internet wirelessly from the TV itself.

- **Wireless**. This involves connecting to the internet directly from the Smart TV. It can either be done during the initial setup process, or from within the settings of the smart TV. During the setup process you will need to have the password that you use to connect devices to your Wi-Fi router. The password is entered using the smart TV's remote control.

- **Wired**. A wired connection can be used for a smart TV, in a similar way to connecting a PC or laptop to the internet. This is done by connecting your smart TV directly to your Wi-Fi router, using an Ethernet cable. It is possible to use adapters to join more than one Ethernet cable if it is in another room from the smart TV, but it is better to have the router in reasonable proximity to the TV.

Amazon Video and Amazon Fire TV Stick

In addition to connecting directly to the internet, content can also be viewed on a smart TV using a TV streaming service. These are offered by companies including Amazon and Apple, and content is streamed to your smart TV using one of their dedicated devices, that attach to the TV.

The Amazon streaming TV service is known as Amazon Video, and it can be accessed through PCs, laptops, smartphones and tablets. It can also be streamed directly to a smart TV. To do this:

1 Buy the Fire TV Stick from the Amazon website

2 Plug the Fire TV Stick into an HDMI port at the back of your TV

3 Follow the onscreen setup process, using the Fire TV Stick remote control to enter details onscreen, such as the Wi-Fi password

4 Content can be selected from the Amazon Video Home screen and navigated with the remote control

Hot tip

Subscribers to the Amazon Prime service automatically have access to a range of Amazon Video content.

179

Don't forget

The TV has to be set to HDMI mode in order to view the Amazon Video content through the Fire TV Stick.

Hot tip

The Amazon Fire TV Stick, and its onscreen content, can be controlled with voice commands, using the supplied remote control or an Amazon Echo.

...cont'd

Apple TV

Apple's video streaming service is known as Apple TV, and it can be used to view content from Apple's iTunes Store and also a range of subscription services including Netflix, Hulu and HBO (subscriptions apply for some services). Apple TV can be used in a similar way to Amazon Video:

1 The Apple TV service is provided by the Apple TV box that connects to a TV using an HDMI port

Apple TV is run by the tvOS operating system, which receives regular software updates through the Apple TV box.

2 Use the remote control to navigate through the content

3 Individual items can be bought and downloaded from the iTunes Store and other services can also be accessed,

including free channels such as YouTube, or subscription ones such as Netflix

11 Looking Forward

This chapter looks at the future for smart homes.

Robots in the Home

Having fully functioning robots in the home may seem like a science fiction vision, but it is a huge area of development in the world of technology, and robots are starting to become a more common feature in the home.

Home robots combine sophisticated engineering, powerful computing capabilities, and Artificial Intelligence (AI) to learn from their environment and adapt their behavior accordingly.

Domestic robots come in various shapes and sizes:

Don't forget

Although robots for the home are relatively expensive, some are definitely affordable and worth looking at by anyone excited about this technology. The one certain thing that can be said about home robots is that the technology will become more powerful and sophisticated over the next few years, and the prices will start to drop significantly.

- **Traditional**. Some devices are designed to appear as a stereotypical robot, based on what many of us have seen in science fiction movies and TV shows. This gives the robots an instantly familiar appearance and appeal.

- **Functional**. Since there is not specific reason why robots should have a particular appearance, some robots are designed with function in mind rather than their outer appearance. These may look more like other computing devices, such as smart speakers.

182

- **Pets**. Robots designed as pets is an area of great interest, as the devices can perform a range of tasks and also provide a level of companionship.

- **Humanoid**. Perhaps one of the most exciting, and contentious, areas of development, robots that try to closely replicate human appearance have already reached a level of sophistication that suggests that in the near future they will be available as companions and helpers around the home. Because of their human appearance, this has raised some misgiving at the thought of the robots evolving to take over from their human masters (see tip).

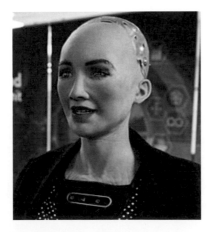

Beware

There are some genuine concerns about the possibility of robots becoming so developed that they begin to act for their own benefit rather than that of their creators. Through the use of AI it is possible that robots could start to develop their own digital thought processes. However, the possibility of them being able to evolve for their own means is still a distant one. Future developments will hopefully include some regulations in relation to the development of AI in robots.

...cont'd

Robot functionality

Robots in the home can be used to perform a range of different tasks, depending on their level of sophistication and power.

- **Domestic chores**. As we have seen in the previous chapter (Chapter 10), robotic devices can be used to cut the grass or vacuum around the home. However, robots can also be used for a range of other domestic chores. These include fetching items, picking up items and replacing them in their original location, turning on domestic appliances, and mopping floors. Robots that are used for fetching and returning items use gripper hands to perform these tasks.

- **Safety.** Domestic robots use AI to recognize certain types of behaviors in humans and learn to react accordingly. For instance, if someone is driving a car and starts to fall asleep, the robot will recognize the change in posture and alert the driver. Similarly, if someone has had a fall at home, the robot will be able to identify that this is not a natural position and send an alert accordingly.

- **Companionship**. Robots such as pet robots are excellent companions for young and old alike. They can be used to mimic the behavior of animal pets and learn from activities that they perform. They can also understand voice commands, and there is a level of unpredictability programmed into them, so that they act more like real pets.

Artificial Intelligence (AI)

Artificial Intelligence (AI) describes a device's ability to study its environment and the tasks that it is asked to do within that environment, and then adapt accordingly. Some of the areas involved in the development of AI include:

- **Natural language processing**. This helps devices react to natural conversation and develop the ability to have two-way dialogs.

- **Reasoning**. This enables devices to look at tasks and problems and try to find a solution themselves.

- **Learning**. This helps devices to evaluate how a task has been performed and correct any errors the next time.

Artificial Intelligence is also sometimes referred to as machine learning.

One of the main objectives of AI is to enable devices to be able to perform tasks and solve problems, without the additional intervention of an external source.

AI is already firmly in operation in a range of areas:

- **Photography**. Some digital cameras use AI for image recognition of individuals and lighting conditions in a photo, and remembering this for future shots.

- **Self-driving cars and drones**. These are being designed so that they can recognize the environment in which they are operating and adapt accordingly. There are a range of safety issues with both self-driving cars and drones.

- **Games**. Chess-playing computers are an example of AI, where the computer learns as it plays the game, in addition to having a database of previous games to refer to.

- **Health**. A lot of research is being undertaken into the use of AI in the diagnoses of a range of diseases. The potential in this area is huge and subject to considerable development.

- **Targeted advertising**. Search engines use AI to look at users' behavior and target advertisements to them accordingly.

AI raises a number of moral and ethical issues, in addition to the technological challenges. As AI develops in the future, it may be up to the policy makers to decide how to use it in wider society and any restrictions that should be placed upon it.

The Smart Home Future

In the world of technology, new developments can be so fast that predicting what may happen in the future can be redundant as it appears as soon as it is predicted. But the future for the smart home is definitely bright, and there are some areas where predictions can be made.

Cost

Although a lot of smart home devices are now affordable for many, it is still relatively expensive to fully equip a home with smart devices. However, most computing technology becomes progressively more powerful and less expensive, e.g. digital cameras, and this will doubtless apply to smart home devices.

Development

Technology never stands still, and the range of smart home devices will undoubtedly expand. Also, existing devices will gain a greater range of functionality as more users demand more features.

Greater acceptance

A lot of new technology can sometimes be seen as unnecessary, and some people may currently view smart home devices in this way. But in the same way that, over the years, we have seen devices such as washing machines, microwave ovens, and TV remote controls become indispensable in the home, it is probable that in a few years no one will question the fact that they control their lights with a voice command or clean their home with a robotic vacuum cleaner.

Security

As with all computing devices, security will become a greater issue as more people use smart home devices. There will almost certainly be a range of security concerns that arise, and a subsequent mushrooming of smart home security software and devices. Security issues have to be seen as the ongoing price to be paid for the convenience of smart home devices. Regulation of smart home devices such as robots in the home may also become an issue as society comes to terms with turning over a lot of everyday tasks to robotic devices.

The smart home of the future may look significantly different from how we currently use smart home devices. However, the journey will be an exciting one that will be filled with new devices and a developing way in which we interact with our homes.

Don't forget

Whatever smart home devices are currently available, it is certain that even more exciting products are already being developed.

Index

T

V

W

Y

Z

31901064597737